ISTANBUL
THE CRADLE OF CIVILISATIONS

MERT
BASIM YAYINCILIK DAĞITIM VE REKLAMCILIK TİC. LTD. ŞTİ.

2 0 0 8

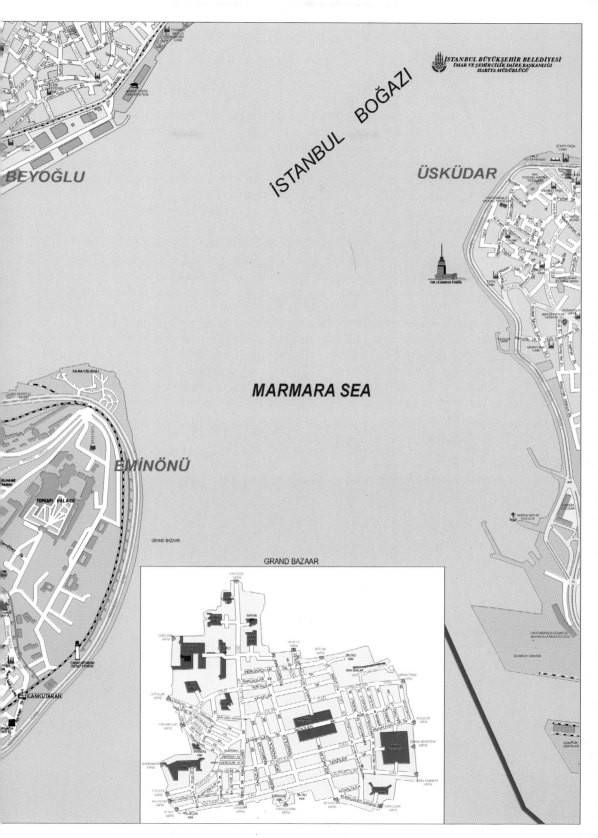

Istanbul

*T*he most important reason why Istanbul has developed as a world metropolis is the geopolitical location of the city. Istanbul, located where the 48. north latitude and 28. east longitude intersect, is the only city in the world which is established on two continents.

The city consists of three parts in general; On the European side, the Historical Peninsula to the south of the Golden Horn and the Galata District to the north, and the New City on the Asian side.

The European side of the city is a trade and business center, whereas the Asian side is more of a residential area. Istanbul is established on the both sides of the Bosphorus, which connects the Black Sea and the Sea of Marmara, and separates Asia and Europe. The 7 km. long narrow inlet, named as the Golden Horn, divides the European side of the city into two. Because of its location between Asia and Europe, the city always had a great geopolitical importance.

Today, Istanbul is still a political and commercial center for the Balkan and Middle Eastern Countries and the Turkic Republics of Central Asia.

The settlement, known as Byzantium after its founder, took the name Constantinople, the city of Emperor Constantine', during the reign of the Roman Emperor Constantine the Great. It was then known as Istanbul after the conquest of the Ottomans, and became one of the biggest and the most crowded city of Europe. The city is spread over an area of 7.500 km², 150 km. long and 50 km. wide.

Süleymaniye Mosque.

Although its population is not occurately known, it is an estimated 12 to 15 million. Because of the continuous immigration from the rural areas, the city grows rapidly and the population increases around half a million every year. Each year, 1.000 new streets are constructed within the city, and brand new settlements rise on the east west axis. The population of the city, with a %5 annual increase, doubles in every 12 years. One out of every five citizens, is living in Istanbul. Around 2 million tourists visit Istanbul every year, and admire the historical and natural beauties of the city. The city has A lots of the finest monuments and museums of Turkey. Istanbul, where East and West, Asia and Europe meets, is a world city that different cultures and religions create the most harmonious synthesis. With particular consideration of historical monuments and cultural richness, Istanbul may only be compared to Rome, which carries so many similar characteristics. In Rome and in Istanbul, which was the capital for both the Byzantine and Ottoman Empires, administrators and governors constructed the greatest religious and civil structures, and decorated their capital cities with the most beautiful works of the famous architects. The Bosphorus is unparalleled for its natural beauties such as the Golden Horn and the Islands. Its moderate climate, active night life, lovely people, and the excellent Turkish Cuisine are some of the other factors, which make Istanbul an attractive destination for the foreigners. A foreigner wishing to know Istanbul closely should spend at least a week in this beautiful city.

History of Istanbul

*T*he earliest traces of settlement around Istanbul are observed on the Asian side and the history of the site extends far back to the Neolithic Age. The first settlement near the Topkapı Palace dates back to the Bronze Age. The Dorians, who escaped from the Megarons, established Khalcedon on the Asian side in 680 BC. Two decades after this, the Megaron colonists came in under their commander Byzas and established the first great settlement in the district called Sarayburnu, the historical peninsula on the European side, right across the settlement on the Asian side. Because of its geographical status and the convenient natural harbor for trade, the city extended beyond and acquired wealth in a short time. In BC 513, the city was captured by the Persians, and in 407 BC, came under the rule of Athens. The Galatians of European origin, settled on the Asian side of the city in 227 BC. A military alliance for defense and security of the city was realized with Rome in 146 BC. In 196, the Roman Emperor Septimus Severus included the city within the territories of the Roman Empire. Emperor Constantine the Great made an extended housing overview throughout the city, renamed the town as Constantinople, and declared to the world with ceremonies (May 11th,

6

Blue Mosque and the Sultanahmet Square.

330) that the city is the second capital for Rome. By the way, strong city walls were constructed around the city. With the efforts of Constantine the Great, who had admitted Christianity under the influence of his deeply Christian mother, this new religion spread in the city and became the state religion in 391. With the death of the Emperor Theodosius I. in 395, the Roman Empire was separated and Constantinople became the capital of East Roman, or the Byzantine Empire. In the early 5th century, the city walls which are still standing today were constructed. Although the West Roman Empire came to the end in 476, the East Roman Empire continued its sovereignty and influence. Between the years of 527 - 565, in the reign of Justinian, many new buildings, the first of which is Hagia Sophia, were constructed. This was the brightest times of the city under the administration of the Byzantine Empire. The Arabs attempted to conquer the city many times from 666 until 870.

The disagreements between the Catholic and Orthodox Church increased and the two churches were separated from each other in 1054. Constantinople became the religious center for the Orthodox. In 1096, the first Crusade passed through without damaging the city. In the 11th and 12th centuries, the Genoese and Venetians mastered the trade especially in the Galata region. In 1204, the Latins came with the 4th Crusade, captured and ruined the city. In 1261 Constantinople was taken over one more time by the Paleologos dynasty. In the late 14th century, the Ottomans started the siege of the city for the first time. The city was besieged by Bayezid I in 1390 and by Murad II in 422, and was conquered by the Ottoman armies commanded by Mehmet II in 1453. The city adopted the name Istanbul and became the 3rd capital of the Ottomans after Bursa and Edirne. In 1517, after the Ottomans conquered Egypt and brought the caliphate to Istanbul, the city became the center of the whole world of Islam.

From 16th century till the stagnation in the 18th, the city was embellished with beautiful mosques, complex and palaces. However, the earthquakes and the fires caused extensive damages in the city. In the 19th century, as a result of the renovation efforts within the Empire, a transition from classical Ottoman architecture to Baroque and Rococo is observed. During the World War I., on the night of March 15th, 1919, the city was captured by the allied armies. After the Independence War was won, and the Sultanate and Caliphate were abolished, the Turkish Republic was declared and Ankara became the capital of the new Republic on October 13th, 1923. After losing the title capital, Istanbul still continued to extend rapidly as the trade and commercial center of Turkey. The city, where shopping centres, cultural buildings and highways were constructed, became a great metropolis, especially in the last 20 years.

Hagia Irene and the Topkapı Palace.

A look from Eminönü to Topkapı Palace.

The Historical Peninsula

The most important places of interest in Istanbul are in Sarayburnu and Sultanahmet regions in the center of the Historic Peninsula. During the Roman Empire, Byzantine and Ottoman periods, the heart of the city was always this region where the palaces of the emperors were built.

The biggest churches, the most glorious mosques and the greatest museums of the city are in this area. Two of the seven hills within the historical peninsula are in this region.

On one of these, the Topkapi Palace, and on the other one Sultanahmet Mosque are placed. Other important historical monuments of the city have been sprinkled here and there on the plains between the hills.

Moreover, the outdoor area that is named as the Hippodrome, which was the center of the city during the Byzantine and Ottoman ages, is also located here. In order to pay a complete visit to the great works such as Hagia Sophia Museum, Topkapı Palace, Sultanahmet Mosque, which are built very near to each other, as well as the Archeological Museum, Museum of Turkish and Islamic Arts and the Mosaic Museum, one should spend at least a couple of days in this area.

The Hagia Sophia Museum.

Hagia Sophia

*H*agia Sophia, which was accepted as the greatest and most sacred piece of the city during the Byzantine age, is today a museum that the visitors admire as an unrivaled architectural masterpiece. Hagia Sophia is a Roman monument constructed in the Byzantine Age. Despite the new techniques and inventions in architecture during the 800 years period from the construction of the church till the demolition of the Empire, no other building could be constructed to surpass Hagia Sophia.

Hagia Sophia, which was used as a church for 916 years since the date it was constructed (537), until the date when Istanbul was conquered. As of this date until the year of 1934, served the Moslems as a mosque for 481 years. After an extended restoration with the instruction given by the founder of the Republic of Turkey, Mustafa Kemal Atatürk, in order to bring the Byzantine mosaics which were coated with stucco in 1750 into daylight, the building was opened to the visitors as a museum in February 1935 and it is the 3rd museum which is most visited in Turkey.

The name Hagia Sophia, is one of the 3 adjectives dedicated to the God in Christianity.

These 3 adjectives are defined as Hagia Sophia (Divine Wisdom), Hagia Irene (Divine Peace) and Hagia Dynamis (Divine Power).

HISTORY

In 360, the Byzantine Emperor Constantine had a great structure named Megalo Ekklesia' (the Great Church), constructed in the city center, where Hagia Sophia is standing today.

Between the years of 404 - 416, a bigger and more lasting church was constructed by the architect Ruffinos on the foundations of this wooden building, which was completely burnt during a fire on June 20th, 404 and it was opened for the public on October 10th, 416. The financier of this second church, with 3 naved basilica design, was Emperor Theodosius. The foundation walls, stairs and the sheep designed pediment friezes of the building just in front of Hagia Sophia are seen at the entrance of the museum. They were irreparably destroyed by the rebels against the Emperor during the sanguinary Nika (Victory) revolt, which began on January 13th and 14th, 532.

After the Nika revolt, Emperor Justinian, who met his throne again, had the present church constructed. He gave the task of con-

The Hagia Sophia and the view of the interior.

The Hagia Sophia and the general view of the interior.

structing this church to the two most famous Anatolian architects of the time, mathematician Anthemius of Tralles (today's Aydın city) and Isidorus from Miletus.

The best construction material and the best masons were brought to the city from all over the country, and for the 5 years, over 100 masters and 10.000 laborers worked in the construction. The marble used for the inner decoration of the church were transported from all the Mediterranean countries, and especially from the marble quarries in Anatolia. The four green granite columns on both sides of the nave were brought from the Harbor Gymnasium in Ephesus, the pairs of porphyry columns at the corners were brought from the Apollon Temple in Baalbek (in Lebanon today).

Special tiles and bricks were brought from the Island of Rhodes in order to built the giant dome with lighter material. A total sum of 107 columns were used in the building and 40 of them are in the nave, the rest 67 in the galleries upstairs.

In the Iconoclastic Era that started in 726, the mosaics concerning the religious scenes and holy personalities of all churches together with Hagia Sophia's were destroyed and simple cross shapes were decorated instead. With the end of this era in 843, religious pictures were allowed again and Hagia Sophia was redecorated with frescoes and mosaics, generally ordered by

The Hagia Sophia and the view of the interior.

the emperors. During the Latin invasion in 1204, the treasury was plundered by the Crusaders.

The mosaics with gold colored background were ruined to a large extend. In this period, Hagia Sophia was used as the Catholic Master Church. When the Latin invaders abandoned the city in 1261, the church came into use as an Orthodox church again. Hagia Sophia was damaged badly because of the earthquakes in 14th and 15th centuries and it was neglected.

Following the conquest, Fatih Sultan Mehmet, performed the Friday service in Hagia Sophia on 3rd of June, 1453. He reserved the necessary fund to restore and save the building.

Hagia Sophia was converted into a mosque. With this fund, first a niche was constructed in the Kaaba direction, then a brick minaret and a madrasah with 12 rooms. A courtyard and a cistern in place of the chamber, where the rooms of the clergy used to be, were constructed outside in front of the building.

The mosaics were covered with thin lime; the cross shapes on the wall were engraved, and vertical sides of the cross shapes on the doors were extracted; by this way, without giving much damage to the building, the place was made suitable for the Moslem service.

The most extended restoration carried out in Hagia Sophia in the Ottoman times was the one made by the Swedish Gaspare and Trajano

FOSSATI brothers between the years of 1847 and 1849. The architects, who came to Istanbul in 1837 in order to repair the Russian Embassy, in respect with the wish of the Ottoman administration, reinforced the dome of Hagia Sophia with 2 chains, adjusted 12 inclined columns, fixed the madrasah, which was destroyed in 1479 and built the cloakroom in the garden. The sultan's lodge inside the nave is the work of the same people.

ARCHITECTURAL DESIGN AND DIMENSIONS

Hagia Sophia, which suits the '3 nave domed basilica' description as an architectural design, is the first construction of this type. Hagia Sophia is also the construction where the 'pendentives' decorated with the drawings of Cherubim angels, from the 14th century, were used for the first time.

The 55.6 m. high dome is one of the 5 highest domes not only in Istanbul and in Turkey, but also in the whole world. After the earthquake in 553, the dome was 6.5 m. heightened and reconstructed between the years of 558 - 562. Since it could not be built round, it has an ellipse shape and the diameter is 31 m. on one axis and 33 m. on the other.

The main area of this total 100 m. long and 7.570 m² large construction is 75 m. to 70 m. The narthex that is located just at the entrance is around 60 m. long, 11 m. wide.

The Hagia Sophia, Emperor Justinianus, Virgin Mary and the Emperor Constantine.

The Hagia Sophia, Deisis Mosaique.

NARTHEXES

There is no ornamentation on the walls and ceiling of this part, which is the preparation place before praying. A few panels of mosaics, which were brought here from various constructions, one tomb brought from Zeyrek and high relief panels of the resolutions decided in the consul held in the 12th century can be seen here.

There are 9 cross shaped arcades on the ceiling which is in a very bad condition because of humidity.

On the inner cornices of the door that provides the passage from the outer narthex to the inner narthex, MDCCCXLVII is written; the date of 1847 with roman figures.

Furthermore, the crosses, whose horizontal axles were extracted in the Ottoman Period, can also be seen on the door folds. The amazingly beautiful ornaments of the construction begin as of the inner narthex. By placing colourful marble panels symmetrically on the wall, the lines of the stones create mystic figures. The ceilings of this part are completely covered with golden mosaics.

A detail from Deisis Mosaique, Jesus Christ.

18

A 16.000 m² area within the construction is decorated with marble paving called Tesserae, and colourful stone pieces. This area is more than two times the total area of the church itself. There are 9 doors for the passage from the inner narthex to the main residence. 3 of these doors, placed on either side, were for public use.

The big door in the very center belonged to the Emperor, and the relatively lower entrances were for the high ranking officials and directors and the escorts, accompanied the emperor.

The golden plating of the Emperor's door and the silver plating of the two doors on both sides of it were taken off during the Latin invasion. Above the Emperor's door, there is a mosaic dated as the 9th century with Jesus Christ in the middle, and in the medallions on the left and right side of it, there are Virgin Mary and Arc Angel Gabriel.

NAVE

Entering the nave from the inner narthex, the first thing that draws the attention is the magnificence of the dome that looks as if it is an independent piece from the church itself. In the center of the dome, around which there are 40 windows, was the painting of Jesus Christ from the Byzantine period.

Emperor Constantin Monumachus IV., Christ and Empress Zoe.

Emperor Comnenos II, Virgin Mary, Jesus Christ and Empress Irene.

After the conquest, the painting was covered with verses of the Koran. On the triangular pendentives which carries the dome and placed between the arches at four corners, there is the pictures of Cherubim angels with 3 wings. The faces of the angels, that are 11 m. long, are in lion, bull, eagle and angel shapes, and each one is covered with one polygonal star.

The portrayals of Ignatios, patriarch of Constantinople in 9th century, 4th century patriarch, John Crysostom, and the patriarch of Antiochia (Antakya today) of 2nd century, Ignatios Theophoros are seen on the side wall under the windows to the left of the entrance. The 1.250 lt. giant marble containers, placed on the left and right side of the entrance are brought from the ancient city of Pergamon in 16th century.

The rectangular marble column placed just at the beginning of the left isle, is named as the 'crying column' or 'sweating column'. It is believed that if you insert your thumb in the hole on the column a little bit damp inside and make one complete circle, the wish comes true.

The Arabic written huge plates on the side walls and the corners, have the names of the leading personalities of Islam.

On the right side of the niche, the name Allah (God), on the left 'Muhammed', on the side walls, the four initial Caliphs of Islam; Ebu Bekir, Ömer, Osman and Ali, and on both sides of the entrance, the grandsons of

the prophet, Hasan and Hüseyin names are placed. These 7.5 m. wide round plates are accepted as some of the greatest examples of calligraphy in the world of Islam. The place to the left of the apse is the Sultan's lodge, while the steps on the right side is the pulpit, where the imam preaches on Fridays. And just in front of the pulpit, there is the Preacher's Throne, which is a 16th century piece of art, and where the Koran is read either in or on it.

The hand print, which is seen on the wall by the red porphyry columns to the right of the apse, is dedicated to Virgin Mary. This marble piece was brought here from Theotokos Church, which is an other Byzantine work in Istanbul. On the right isle, there is the Hagia Sophia Library, which was moved from the Palace Library in the reign of Sultan Mahmut 1. in the 18th century.

The mosaic panel, which is the best protected one in the church, is over the side door of the inner narthex, that the emperors used as the entrance in the Byzantine period, whereas it is used as the exit today.

In this panel there is Virgin Mary seated on a throne in the center with baby Christ. The Emperor Constantine is on the right, and Emperor Justinian on the left. In the hands of Constantine the Great, there is the model of the city and in Justinian's, there is the model of the church. Both emperors dedicated their proud works to Virgin Mary and Jesus Christ.

GALLERIES

You can reach the upper floor, that was used by the women during the service and the consuls, with an inclined thoroughfare to the left of the inner narthex.

This structure was preferred instead of stairs by the order of the queen, who was praying with the other women, in order not to disturb the queen as she was carried on shoulders with a litter to the upstairs.

The cross shaped wooden stretchers between the arcades in the central gallery, just to the opposite side of the niche, are elegant hand made artifacts, that you can only find similar ones in the Catherina Monastery in Sina Desert.

The south gallery to the right side of the entrance is the most attractive part of the upper galleries.

On the marble panels at the left hand side, there are the writings that are described as a hearsay remained from the Vikings, who visited Istanbul. The engraved marble portal at the entrance of the right wing of the gallery is named as the 'Heaven's Door'. At the back side of this portal, you can see two cross motives.

When you pass through the portal on the right side, there is probably the most beautiful and most attractive mosaic of Hagia Sophia.

Very fine and colourful mosaic tiles were used for this scene, in which Jesus Christ, Mother Mary and John the Baptist appears together, although this panel suffered great damage during the Latin invasion, the mosaics still has a very high artistic value.

The scene named as Deisis' dates back to 14th century and depicts Mother Mary and John the Baptist asking Jesus Christ, in grief, for the sinful to be sent to heaven.

At the end of the gallery, there are two other mosaic panels with different emperors and their families depicted together with holy personalities. Emperor Comnenos, his Hungarian originated wife Irene and their son Alexius are portrayed with Virgin Mary and baby Christ in her arms.

On the panel to the left, on the other hand, Christ is seated on a throne, and Empress Zoe and her third husband Constantine Monomachos are on both sides. In this mosaic, where the empress had been depicted with his first husband Romanos III in the 11th century the first time, it is recognizable that the name and the head of the emperor in the scene was changed after each marriage of the empress.

At the furthest point of the gallery, when you look at the upper part of the apse, you can see the mosaic, where Virgin Mary and baby Christ are pictured with the archangels Michael and Gabriel (9th century).

Yerebatan Cistern

*T*he entrance of the Underground (Yerebatan) Cistern, which is the biggest of over sixty cisterns built in Istanbul during the Byzantine Period, is just across from Hagia Sophia Museum.

Since there were not enough water sources inside the Byzantine ramparts that surrounded the city, for ages, the water of the city was supplied from the rivers and sources in the Belgrade Forest, which is 25 km. north of Istanbul.

During the wars and sieges, as the enemy soldiers used to destroy the ducts bringing water to the city or poison the water, large cisterns were constructed for storing water since the very beginning.

Various views from the Underground Cistern (Yerebatan Sarnıcı).

Yerebatan Cistern, which was completed in a very short time (only a couple of months) in 532, is the storage where the water was delivered to the city through the Valens Aquaduct, is stored. It was used until the 16th century. The cistern, which was in use for a short period of time during the Ottoman Period, was restored in the mid 19th century.

The cistern, where columns from different Roman structures were used, is 70 m. wide, 140 m. long, with a total sum of 336 columns, which were placed in every 4 m. The total water capacity of the cistern is 80.000 m³ and its height is 8 m. and has around 10.000 m² surface area.

After the restoration work completed in 1987, the cistern was opened for the public visit. The lights and classical music played complete the mystic atmosphere in the cistern.

At the very back side, the two Medusa heads, which are used as column bases, are placed side way down whereas the other one is placed upside down. Certain scenes of the James Bond movie named 'From Russia with Love' was filmed in Yerebatan Cistern.

The Blue Mosque
(Sultan Ahmet Mosque)

Sultan Ahmet Mosque, which was constructed by the 14th Ottoman Sultan Ahmet I, who ruled between the years of 1603 - 1617, is the greatest and the most splendid mosque of Istanbul. The construction of the mosque was started in 1609 by architect Mehmet Agha, who was a student of Architect Sinan and who undertook the architectural works of the structure and the construction was completed in 1616. The premises consisted of a madrasah, a hospital, an Arasta Bazaar, a school, a mausoleum, a caravansary and a public fountain together with the mosque. The hospital and the caravansary were damaged in 19th century.

Sultan Ahmet Mosque is the last impressive structure of Ottoman religious architecture. Although many other mosques were built after this one, none of them reached to the dimension and to the elegance of the decorations of Sultan Ahmet Mosque.

The land preferred for the mosque construction was the old Hippodrome, known as Atmeydanı, and was the center of the city since the Byzantine Period. During the preparation of the huge area, many earlier Byzantine and Ottoman structures had to be demolished to open a space for the construction. Among these structures, the Royal Byzantine Palace,

The Blue Mosque.

Blue Mosque.

remains of the auditorium of the Hippodrome, and palaces of many Ottoman dignitaries can be listed. Its close proximity to the Topkapı Palace was the reason why this area was chosen for the mosque. A very careful selection was made for the construction and decoration material.

The 21.043 tile pieces used for the inner decoration of the mosque were brought from the palace workshops in İznik, the silk carpets on the floor of hundreds of square meters were brought from selected weaving centers, and hundreds of crystal oil lamps used for illumination were imported. It is known that the leading administrators of the state donated many valuable gifts, especially the handwritten Korans after the completion of the mosque.

The dimensions of the front courtyard, constructed on a podium arising in the middle of the outer courtyard and the dimensions of the main nave are almost the same size, and it is 72 m. x 64 m. wide. There are five doors for entrance opening into the outer courtyard. Among these doors, there is a chain hanging above the main entrance. According to the legend, the reason why this chain was hung, was to have the sultan, who came to the mosque on his horse, to get off his horse and walk in with respect like anyone else. There are three portals that provide access to the inner courtyard, as you climb up the stairs.

The Blue Mosque, interior view.

There are taps used for ablutions below the north portico of the front court-yard. Furthermore, there is a fountain for ablutions in the middle of the court-yard with 6 corners and 6 columns. 30 small size domes are constructed on a total 26 granite columns.

Sultan Ahmet Mosque is the only mosque with 6 minarets in Istanbul and in Turkey, and that make it matchless among other Ottoman Mosques. The minarets placed at the corners of the mosque and the courtyard have a total of 16 balconies. Certain sections of some minarets are embellished with blue tiles. According to the legend about the minarets of the mosque, Sultan Ahmet I asked from the architect, Mehmet Ağa, a mosque with a golden minaret. Because of the turkish pronunciation of gold is dike to number six, architect Mehemet Ağa misunderstood this point, so, the architect preferred a mosque with 6 minarets instead of golden ones, as the cost would be very high. The dimensions of the nave, which is almost square planned, are 51 m. x 53 m. The Architect Mehmet Ağa has no sig-nificant innovations in the plan and design of the Ottoman mosques in the Classical Period from the architectural point of view, but the inner decoration of the mosque has the specifications of being eclipsed of the previous Ottoman Mosques. Essentially, the reason why the mosque is known as the 'Blue Mosque' all over the world is because of the tiles and embellishments, which are mostly in blue and green colors on the walls and the domes.

The Blue Mosque.

The carpet weaving showed progress in Moslem world, as the namaz is performed on the floor; whereas the carpet works did not improve in Christianity, because the service is followed by the attendants that are seated. Manufacturing tiles is one of the handicrafts that the Turks dealt with since the 12th century. Just like in carpet weaving, in manufacturing tiles, every region has its own design and color differences. The most frequently used designs in the mosques are springs, leaves, calyxes, tulips, roses, hyacinths, carnations, pomegranate flowers and grapes, and geometric patterns to a certain extend.

When you look at the building from the exterior, the structure forms an elegant scene that you never expect from its dimensions.

The main dome, the arches supporting it, all round and angular carrier architectural elements are set up in a complete harmony. All edges and corners, which would not look nice, are rounded, the big carrier elements are softened in a complete sense. The light coming in through the windows placed around the dome, together with the windows covered with stain glass in 5 rows especially through the apse wall, intensifies the beauty of the tiles and decorations. There are total 260 windows in the mosque. The Venetian glasses, which were used in the first construction of the mosque, unfortunately could not stay until today. The diameter of the 43 m. high dome reaches to 23.5 m. The diameter of the giant buttresses called elephant feet, which are carrying this giant dome and the elements surrounding it together with the pendentives, is about 5 m. Under two of these columns, which are nearby the entrance, there are taps for

The Blue Mosque.

ablutions. The old writings embellishing the walls and columns together with the central dome of the mosque and the conches are the works of an artist named Seyid Kasım Bubari from Diyarbakır and these are various verses of Koran and the substantial sayings of Prophet Mohammed.

Until a recent time, the precious handmade carpets in various colors and design, which completely covered the entire floor of the mosque were unfortunately exchanged with machine made carpets.

The wood benches in the mosque were placed to leave the shoes on, in case there is no place at the outer shelves. The galleries at the three sides of the mosque, except the wall pointing south-east, are for the use of women and religious meetings.

The monumental burial in front of the mosque was built by Sultan Osman II, son of Sultan Ahmet I, in it there is the grave of Sultan Ahmet I, besides the graves of Osman II and Murat IV. Moreover, Kösem Mahpeyker Sultan, wife of Ahmet I and whom was loved so much by him, is also buried at the same place. Other than these, there are thirty two more burials belonging to the royal family members.

Mosaic Museum

*I*nside the Arasta Bazaar which is at the backside of Sultanahmet Mosque and which was constructed with the aim of covering the expenses of the mosque out of the rents, there is the Mosaic Museum, where the mosaics dating from the 4th and 6th centuries are exhibited. The museum is located in the halls and court-yards of an old Byzantine Palace, which is placed on a land that beginning from Sultan Ahmet Mosque and reaching the sea, the archeological excavations of it are not fully finished. The most frequently used designs of the mosaics are hunting and mythological scenes, games, wild animal pictures and daily events.

Views from the Mosaique Museum.

Sultanahmet Square, Hippodrome.

Hippodrome The Sultan Ahmet Square

Hippodrome, today named Sultanahmet Square, is the heart of the Old Town. The ancient works in the middle of this square and the structures arranged in a line around the square are the most spectacular historical remains of Istanbul. The Hippodrome's construction was started in 203 during the reign of Septimus Severus just after the Roman conquest of the city. It was finally completed on May 11, 330 for the ceremonies of Byzantine Emperor Constantine the Great, who wished to make this city a second capital for the Roman Empire. The seating capacity was 30.000 spectators obtained in forty rows of seats around the 'U' shaped race track. Hippodrome with 400 m. length and 120 m. width was one of the biggest hippodromes of the antique world after Cicus Maximus in Rome.

Since the land was not flat, the west side of the hippodrome was elevated on a retaining wall. When you approach to the square from the coast of Marmara Sea, these walls called 'sphendone' can be seen with all their magnificence. Furthermore, in the middle of the 'U' shaped race track, there was bumper called 'spina' embellished with works of art. The Hippodrome, where the sportive activities took place was also the stage for riots, public entertainments, social appear-

ances of the royals, wedding ceremonies and bazaars. In the Byzantine Period, the place had three functions. First of these was the sportive activities and art events. Horse-races was an attractive sports event of those times. Other than these, gladiator fights used to be held here. The second function of the Hippodrome was that it was a political arena. In the Ottoman Period the Janissary Corps riots generally started here.

The third function of the square was the decorative purpose as an open - air museum by being embellished richly by the Byzantine Emperors. The spina in the middle displayed, columns, statues, sun clocks, obelisks and monuments brought to the Hippodrome from all over the world.

DIKILITAŞ (OBELISK)

It is not only the Hippodrome's, but also Istanbul's oldest monument. It is dated as 15th century BC; that is to say, this obelisk is 3.500 years old. The Pharaoh made it built for the memory of his victory. There are similar ones in Egypt and in many other big cities of Europe. In BC 390, the Byzantine Emperor Theodosius I brought it from Amon Temple of Karnak in the Luxor region in Egypt and it was erected in its present place of today.

Hippodrome, a miniature of the 16th. Century.

The Egyptian Obelisque.
The Constantine Obelisque.

View of Sultanahmet Square, Hippodrome.

Although in every 100 years average 6.5 scale earthquakes hit the city of Istanbul, it has been standing here for the past 1600 years without getting any damage. It is made from pink granite and its weight is about 300 tons. Although the original was 32.5 m. high, %40 of the bottom was cut off for transportation. It is 20 m. high today. On each four faces of the Obelisk, there are Egyptian Hieroglyphics that tells about the bravery of Pharaoh Tuthmose. At the top, God Amon and the pharaoh were pictured hand in hand. The hawk named Horus below symbolizes the beginning of the text. Some human figures were destroyed, and also some letters below were cut from the center. The reason why the bottom of the obelisk is not flat is because there are 4 bronze feet under it. It is known that water games were held in the water canals attached to the feet. And at the very bottom, there is a marble base constructed in 389. On every four faces of this base, there are scenes from the activities, taken place in the Hippodrome. Many reliefs such as the Emperor's lodge, erecting the Obelisk, dancing before the races, horse-races, Emperor receiving gifts were carved on the marble base.

THE SERPENTINE COLUMN

This second oldest monument in the Hippodrome is dated as BC 479 and it is the Serpentine Column brought from the Apollon Temple in Delphi, Greece by Constantine in 326 and was placed here. This monument symbolizes the victory of the Greek States against Persians in Palatea and its original form consists of a giant golden trophy with of diameter 2

m. and which is set on the heads of three snakes wrapped around each other. Before bringing it to Istanbul, the trophy was lost and the heads of the snakes were broken with stones during the Ottoman Period. One of these heads is exhibited in the Archeological Museum of Istanbul and the other in British Museum in London. The original height was 6.5 m., and is 5 m. today.

COLUMN OF CONSTANTINE:

This last column that was built by Emperor Constantine VII, nicknamed as Porphyrogentus, for the memory of his grandfather, Basileus, was located just in the center of the Hippodrome Square. The Column, dated as the 10th century, is 32 m. high, and was covered with embroidered copper and brass plates and these plates were removed during the Latin invasion in the early 13th century and coins were made out of these equipment. The column, which was heavily damaged by the earthquake in 1894, was restored recently.

GERMAN or KAISER WILHELM FOUNTAIN:

The German Fountain, which is the last and the latest work in the Hippodrome Square, is dated as 1898. The German Emperor, who was impressed by the hospitality that he experienced in Istanbul during his second trip had built this elegant fountain, whose project was prepared by himself on his return to his country. The fountain, which was sent to Istanbul by train, was reassembled in the Hippodrome, Atmeydanı with its present name.

The German Fountain.
A detail from the Obelisque, the
Serpentine Column.

39

Views from Turkish and Islamic Arts Museum.

Museum of Turkish and Islamic Arts

The building at the edge of the Hippodrome, just opposite of the Sultanahmet Mosque, is the Ibrahim Pasha Palace which was the only palace owned by a dignity outside the dynasty in the Ottoman Period. The building was presented by Sultan Süleyman the Magnificent to his Grand Vizier Ibrahim Pasha in 1520.

Following the death of Pasha, the building which was used as the new recruits barracks, palace of embassy, fiscal office, tailoring workshop and prison, and it remained vacant for quite a long time and fell into ruins. The building was restored in 1970's and in 1983 the Museum of Turkish and Islamic Arts was transferred here, from its original location, the Süleymaniye complex. The collection, which includes hand-written books and works made of stone, ceramic, wood and metal, was awarded by the Council of Europe in 1984 and by UNESCO in 1985. The most valuable collection of the museum is handmade Turkish carpets of incredible sizes. The authentic life style and handicrafts of Anatolia are exhibited in this museum with a contemporary museum approach. Drinking a cup of Turkish coffee in a typical Turkish coffee-house, situated in the courtyard of the museum would revive oneself.

Sokollu Mosque.

Sokollu Mosque

*B*efore leaving the Hippodrome Square, it would be beneficial to visit Sokollu Mosque which can be reached going down the path from the western corner of the square.

The Serbian originated wife of Sokollu Mehmet Pasha (who served as the Grand Vizier for three sultans the first of whom was Kanuni and Esmahan Sultan), the daughter of Selim II, had famous Turkish architect Sinan construct this mosque between the years of 1571-1572.

Sokollu Mosque is a small but delightful Ottoman monument worth seeing with its elevated dome of 22 m., 56 windows supplying light for the interior, samples of calligraphy on navy blue and colourful İznik tiles.

Topkapı Palace, Gate of Royal Reception.

Topkapı Palace

*A*s the administrative center, for nearly 400 years, for the Ottoman Empire, which was one of the greatest empires of the world, Topkapı Palace is certainly the most important historical site to be visited in Istanbul. That is the reason why Topkapı Palace is one of the most frequently visited museums of Europe, and is the most visited one in Turkey with a number of more than 2,5 million visitors per year.

After the conquest of Istanbul by the Turks in 1453, the Ottoman Sultan Fatih Sultan Mehmet, who stayed in a rather small palace for a while near the Grand Bazaar, in the district of Bayezıd, constructed the structures that formed the essence of Topkapı Palace on the ruins of ancient Roman city, between the years of 1475-1478. In the following centuries, all the Ottoman Sultans enriched and widened the palace with new structures until it was abandoned in the 19th century.

The original name of the palace used to be 'Saray-ı Cedide-i Amire', however, because of the huge cannons in front of the doors of the palace, the public gave the name 'Topkapı', and this name was commonly used by the locals. The palace, surrounded with walls, around five kilometers, has a total area of around 700.000 m² which is twice the area of Vatican and half of

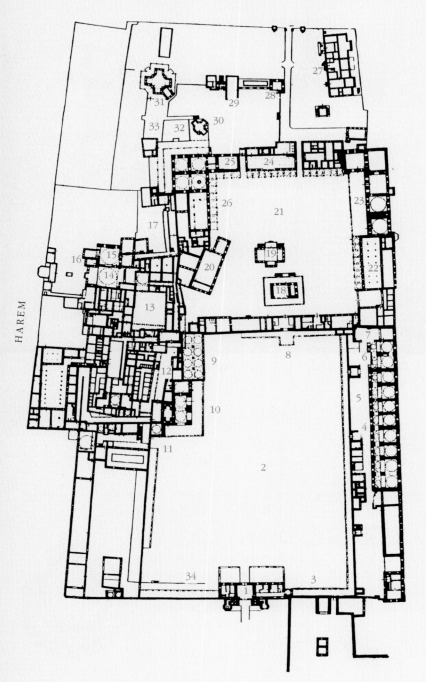

HAREM

PLAN OF TOPKAPI PALACE

1 - Main gate (Babü's selam)
2 - The 2ⁿᵈ courtyard.
3 - Chariots Section.
4 - Chinese and Japanese porcelain Section.
5 - The European Porcelain Section.
6 - Palace Kitchenware Section (helvahane).
7 - Istanbul Glassware and Porcelain Section.
8 - The Akağalar Gate.
9 - The Weapons Section.
10 - The Kubbealtı.
11 - Entrance to the Harem.
12 - The Courtyard of the Karaağalar.
13 - The Courtyard of the Valide Sultan.
14 - The Hünkâr Sofrası.
15 - The Room of Sultan Murat III.
16 - The Fruit Room.
17 - The Courtyard of the Favorites.
18 - Audience Chamber.
19 - Library of Ahmed III.
20 - The Library (Ağalar Mosque).
21 - The 3ʳᵈ courtyard.
22 - Textiles and Kaftans Section.
23 - The Treasury section.
24 - The Inscriptions, Miniatures and Sultans' Portraits Section.
25 - The Clocks Section.
26 - The Sacred Relics Section.
27 - The Mecidiye Pavilion.
28 - Hekimbaşı Tower.
29 - The Sofa Pavilion.
30 - The Revan Pavilion.
31 - The Bagdat Pavilion.
32 - Pool.
33 - The Circumcision Room.
34 - The Bookstore.

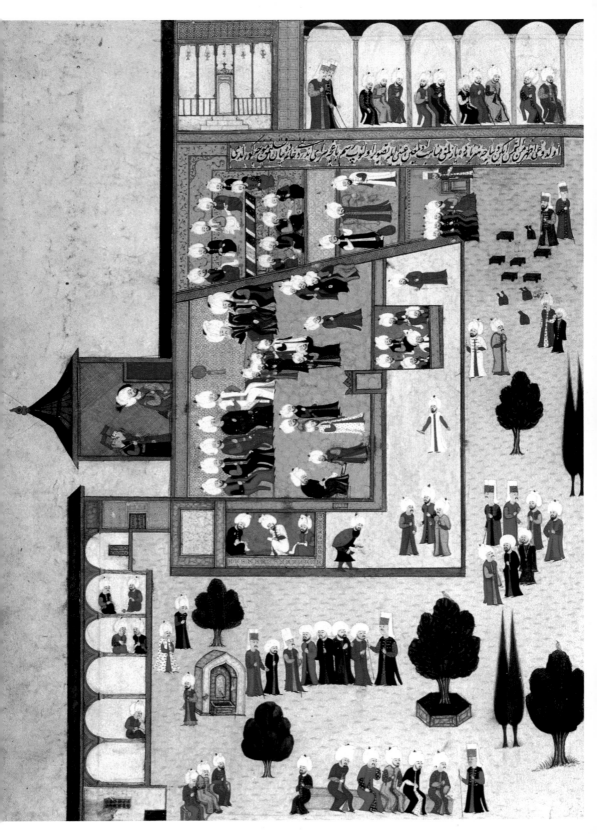

Sultan Selim the 3rd in front of the gate of White Eunuchs.

Monaco in size. The palace was protected by 28 towers. The surrounding city walls along the coast date from the Byzantine period, and the land walls are the work of the Ottomans. There are three entrances on the sea and four on the opposite.

Nearly 5.000 visitors per day visited the palace where approximately 5.000 people who were members of Dynasty, dignitaries, ruling class, maidservants and soldiers lived. Most of the buildings in the palace were destroyed in the big fires and earthquakes which took place frequently in the 16th and 17th centuries and they were restored for a few times. For this reason, different architectural styles of different periods from 15th to 16th may be observed. The general architectural plan of the Topkapı Palace, which is composed of two parts, one of which is ENDERUN, where the Sultan and members of the dynasty lived and the other BIRUN, where high level civil servants manage the works of the government does not resemble to the classical architecture of European palaces. Even though wide and long building including hundreds of rooms and wide gardens behind and in front of the building form the general style of European palaces, Ottomans have preferred quite a different style. Ottomans, who had a nomadic life until a few centuries before the construction of Topkapı Palace, have reflected nomadic traditions to

Sultan Süleyman the Magnificent and Sultan Selim II.

palace architecture as well. Just as the nomads pitch their tents around a vacant area in order to eat and have fun, Ottomans while constructing Topkapı Palace, left great gardens in the middle and constructed palace buildings around them.

When we come to the main entrance after going around the Hagia Sophia, the door we meet is Bab-ı Hümayün Door. In front of this door, the splendid fountain building on the right was constructed in 1728 by Sultan Ahmet III. In the Ottoman times, sherbet (fruit sweet drink) was sold in the small shops located at the sides of this building which was attracting attention with its five domes and tasteful embroideries. Passing through the Bab-ı Hümayün, constructed by Fatih Sultan Mehmet in 1478, visitors face the wide and long 'first courtyard'. On the right side of this courtyard, one can see gendarme station, park areas, dwellings of palace servants, ruins of palace hospital and palace bakery and behind, Marmara Sea. On the left side appear Church of St. Irene and the old Ottoman treasury, and far behind is the Istanbul Archaeological Museums. St. Irene and Archaeological Museums will be introduced in detail in the following chapters.

Through the first courtyard and the ticket office, we pass through the 'BAB-US SELAM' the second main door of the palace and begin our visit in the museum. This door which was constructed during the reigns of Mehmet II is also called as the Central Door. The tower to the left of the door, which was made of wrought iron in 1524 was also used as a prison for those high level servants, who committed a crime during the Ottoman period. There is a myth that executioners used to wash their swords under the fountain in front of the door after executing death sentence.

When we pass through Bab-üs Selam, the courtyard we face is a huge garden 130 m. in width and 160 m. in length, full of very old cypress and plain trees. The small scale models of the palace just by the entrance of this court-yard give the visitors a good idea about the size of the palace. Also, the maps hung on the walls reveal the expansion of the empire during its establishment and rising. The section to the right side of the entrance displays the sultan's chariots.

When the sultan was in the palace, it was forbidden to talk at the 2nd courtyard surrounded with one-floor build-ings, although it was open for the foreigners and the people who came for seeing divan or kitchens. There were gazelles, peacocks and some other exotic animals wandering in the garden which was cared by hundreds of gardeners, it was almost like a Eden Garden. The complete right wing of the second courtyard was the 'palace kitchen'.

KITCHENS AND PORCELAIN COLLECTION :

Nearly 1.200 personnel were working in the palace kitchens which were first constructed in the times of Mehmet II, then restored by famous Turkish architect 'Sinan' in the times of Selim II in the 16th century. When we consider the number of personnel working in all parts of the palace as 5.000, nearly 25 % of this number were serving for kitchen. In the kitchen complex, there were three sections for the sultan, other personnel and the desserts; dormitories of the personnel, mosque, bath and pantry were also here. Each of the ten rooms form-ing the kitchen building were used to cook for various per-sons and groups like the queen mother, the concubines, the crown prince and the black eunuchs.

The domes on the main kitchen building were constructed in the 15th cen-tury and are one of the palace symbols. The chimneys above the domes were constructed by Sinan after the big fire in 1574. Everyday 20.000 meals were pre-pared in the kitchens.

Chinese Porcelains.

That is, other than the three meals for 5.000 people living in the palace, meals for 5.000 people were distributed each day for caravansaries and soup kitchens.

Today, a large part of the kitchen complex hosts the third largest porcelain collection of the world. After the collections of China, Beijing and Germany, Meissen comes the collection of Topkapı Palace Museum which composes of 12.000 pieces. However, only one fourth of this collection, nearly 3.000 works can be displayed.

When we go through the kitchen, porcelains are exhibited chronologically, starting from the times of Tang Dynasty (7th - 9th century), Seladon Dynasty (10th - 12th century) and Ming Dynasty (14th - 17th century) respectively from right to left. At the end of the collection, we observe Japanese porcelains which appeared from 17th century on after those famous Chinese workshops were closed and European porcelains produced in Sevr, Vincent, Meissen, Berlin and Warsaw in the 18th and 19th centuries.

In the 'helvahane' located just beside the sitting rooms where porcelain collections are displayed, huge cauldrons and other kitchen utensils are exhibited. Objects made of glass which were produced in Istanbul Glass Workshops (manufactured only for the palace) and in Venice are displayed at the far corner of the corridor which is besides the helvahane and this corner was once used for making soap and oil. To the opposite side of the corridor you may see the silver souvenirs which were brought to the palace or made by masters in the palace.

HAREM :

The word 'harem' which comes from the Arabic word 'haram' having the meaning of 'forbidden by religion' is the word describing the place where the sultan and his family live. Harem, which is a worldly application of heaven full of beauties that is promised to religious men by Islam, was an inseparable part of the Ottoman Dynasty since it was founded. After Topkapı Palace was constructed, all the government moved to this new palace, however, families of the sultans continued to live in the ancient palace in Bayezıd for nearly 80 years. During the reign of Kanuni Sultan Süleyman, the sultan's family was moved to wooden buildings constructed in Topkapı Palace due to the pressure of Hürrem Sultan, second wife of the sultan, after a fire took place in the ancient palace. Then the influence of the harem

Chinese Porcelains.

49

Harem, the Royal Hall.

and sultan's wives living here began to increase over the government and the sultan.

Many new buildings were constructed instead of the wooden buildings that were completely destroyed during the big fire took place in 1666, and so a complex of buildings consisting nearly 300 rooms, only small part of which is open to visits, appeared. All the buildings we see today were constructed in 16th and 18th centuries. In order to visit the Harem, which was first opened to visits in 1971, one should buy a ticket from the ticket office in the second courtyard and participate the tours which are held in every 30 minutes with local guides providing service in various languages. The tour begins from the exit door of the Harem which was once used for chariots.

Harem was isolated from the outside world, and entrance was a privilege allowed for only the closest relatives of the sultan and people working here. In some certain days, men only from three profession groups had the permission to enter definite rooms of the Harem. These were the doctors who came to control patients, teachers of princes and musicians who were called at the ceremonies. Non-Moslems were certainly not allowed.

Other than the sultan's wives and mother, also brothers and children who were prepared for the throne or who were kept at a distance from the throne and those women and men, who served for this big family, used to stay in the

Harem, the Royal Hall.

Harem. While some sultans were having intercourse with only four women as it is allowed in Islam, some had hundreds of women in the harem. For instance, it is said that there were nearly 1200 women in the harem of Murat III, the first sultan who spent all his time with women' ignoring the state works. 'Concubines' in charge of serving the sultan in the Harem were young girls who were brought from the conquered countries.

They were subject to a rough trainee in the palace after changing their names and converting religions. Those who had children from the sultan after having an intercourse with him were taken to special rooms in the harem. Others would either kept on living there and serve the imperial family by taking another duty in the harem, or by set marriages get married to a high level civil servant.

Almost all women living in the harem including wives of the sultan and the servants were either enslaved, or bought from slave merchants, or presented to the sultan and later became Moslems. These women of distinguished beauty, taken to Istanbul from all parts of the world, were very close to the sultan and gave him children, however, they were not always faithful to the sultan and the Ottoman Dynasty since they had a glittering prison life. These women, who were sentenced to live in the Harem and whose families had been enslaved or killed by the Ottomans, sometimes had not spared to undertake the leading roles in the intrigues against the sultan. In spite of the magnificent image of the palace, the women here were actually living in a competitive atmosphere. Since sultanate passes from father to the elder son in the Ottoman Dynasty, aim of all concubines was giving birth to the first son of the sultan and so becoming 'haseki' (favorite wife) of the sultan. That was the only way of guaranteeing their future. On the other hand, it was not sufficient to be the mother of the first son, as this son had to stay alive until the sultan dies. Some concubines would sometimes try to kill other sons in order to make hers ascend the throne. Also, there were bickers between the favorites of the sultan and his mother (queen mother), who was the absolute master of Harem and second important person after the sultan regarding influencing the empire administration. The Queen Mother was the absolute master of Harem and had nearly 40 rooms and several servants for herself.

Except for nearly 300 rooms, there were 46 toilets, 8 Turkish baths, 4 small kitchens, 2 mosques, 6 pantries, a swimming pool and a hospital in the Harem which was built on a total area of 6.700 m². The Harem is usually composed of 3 large courtyards and rooms surrounding them. These rooms belonged to the Queen Mother, wives of the sultan and the crown prince, to the concubines

Harem, the Chamber of Princes.

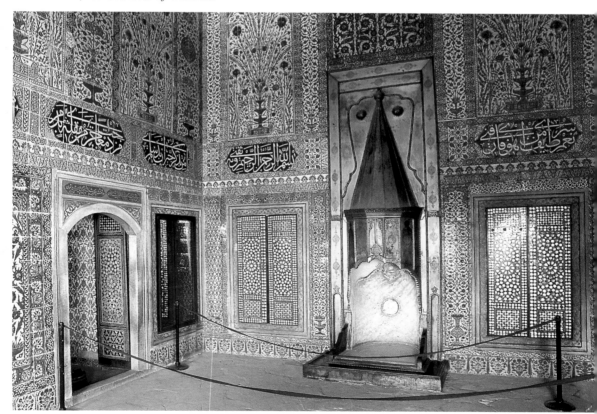

and to 'Black Eunuchs' responsible for protecting the harem. Black Eunuchs were very strong black men who were taken captive during the wars in Africa as slaves or bought from slave merchants. There were about forty of them living in the Harem and they had duties demanding man power.

Chief Black Eunuch was the third most important person after the sultan and Queen Mother. During the tour with a local guide in the Harem, visitors may see everything at a close range: rooms of the black eunuchs, the tiled courtyard, the school of the Crown Prince, courtyard of the sultan's wives apartments and the rooms surrounding, embroidered bed of the Queen Mother, dinner and divine service rooms, marble Turkish bath of the sultan who preferred it because of security, bedroom of Sultan Abdulhamit who reigned in the 18th century, splendid throne room of Murat III who reigned in the 16th century, elegant library of the sultan Ahmet I, dining room of Ahmet III (the walls of this room which is called 'Yemiş Odası' are decorated with the most beautiful ·floral motifs), small rooms in which sultan's brothers lived for years and 'the golden way' of 46 m. where met the sultan and his concubines.

Although the exit of the Harem is in the 3rd courtyard, let us observe the second courtyard more before the third one and give some short information about a few buildings in this courtyard. The building just beside the entrance door of the Harem is called KUBBEALTI (The Dome), the administration center of the Ottoman Empire. The viziers, who got together and chaired by the grand vizier

A view of the tiles of Harem.
Musicians in the Harem.

53

Kiosk of Sultan Abdülhamid I.

four days a week, took important decisions about internal and foreign policy in this large embroidered room. The room behind the caged window located at the upper part of the large room was planned to enable the sultan to watch the meetings without being seen by the viziers. The Dome was also used for the negotiations of statesmen with the foreign ambassadors.

The tower (forty one meters in height), located just above The Dome, was called 'THE JUSTICE TOWER' and constructed as a watch-tower and has become one of the architectural symbols of not only the palace, but also of Istanbul in the following years.

The part used as Foreign Treasury in the Ottoman times and located beside The Dome is used as THE EXHIBITION OF ARMORY. In the previous ages, taxes received from various regions used to be kept here and the wages used to be paid every three months from here. The most important pieces of the armory are the swords of Mehmet II (the conqueror) and Muaviye (one of the Islam commanders), horse armour of Yavuz Sultan Selim, who conquered Middle East, many foreign guns and rifles, swords of executioners, Iranian and Turkish arrow and bow sets and other swords, pikes and armors, which are dated between the 16th - 19th. centuries.

The Dining room of Sultan Ahmed III.

Gate of white Eunuchs (Akağalar Kapısı). Justice Tower.

Passing through the 2nd courtyard to the 3rd, the door facing us is named BABUSSADED or AKAGHALAR DOOR and is the third largest door of the palace. For 400 years the most important ceremonies were made in front of this door, which divides the administration area of the palace from the residential area of the sultan. Enthroning ceremonies of the new sultans, the army's being accompanied for a state of warfare, celebration of the new conquests, rewarding janissaries used to be held under the roof supported by six columns in front of this door. During the ceremonies Ottoman flag was put into the stone hole in the middle, sultan's throne was put in front of it and all high level civil servants and commanders took their place around this door forming a shape of a semicircle.

When we pass through the Babussaded, the first building which faces us in the third courtyard is the one embellished with rich tiles named 'ARZ ODASI'. There is a throne and a fountain on the wall at the left corner of this reception hall, where the decisions taken at the Dome meetings are offered to the sultan and where foreign ambassadors were welcomed with ceremonies. The splashing sound of the fountain, which was turned on during private negotiations, avoided the unwanted listeners. The yellow, green and turquoise tiles on the walls are the finest examples of the Ottoman tile art. The designs of these tiles are often seen on the classical Turkish hand-made carpets as well. Arabic-written wall panels and sultan's monograms can be seen on the walls just opposite to the reception hall.

The building to the right side of the third courtyard entrance was the ancient palace school, however it is now used as the office of the museum management. The first collection on the right wing of the courtyard is THE EXHIBITION OF TEXTILES in the room named 'Seferliler Koğuşu' (Travelers' Dormitory). Costumes of the Ottoman Sultans, Crown Princes and other valuable cloths are exhibited here. Fatih Kiosk near this collection, a building with two large domes, holds THE IMPERIAL TREASURY which is one of the most interesting parts of the palace.

IMPERIAL TREASURY :

This group of buildings, which had been used to conceal palace treasuries in the previous times, was used as the Imperial Treasury Building from the 17th century during the Ottoman era. In the 19th century this treasury was open for the visits of the high positioned European guests and the works of art were exhibited with pride. Systematically exhibited works after the palace converted into a museum in 1924, reveal the richness of the Ottoman Empire. A great majority of the valuable works displayed in the Imperial Treasury Department are the works of palace jewelry masters. For instance, it is known that, in the 15th century, 70 jewelry masters worked in the palace. Nowadays, Turkish jewelry art, under the leadership of the Armenian masters living in Istanbul,

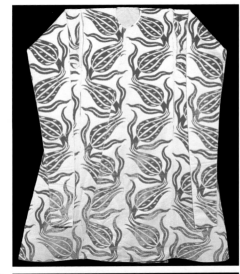

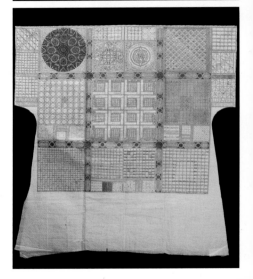

Costumes (Kaftans) of the Sultans.

has the appreciation of the world. Moreover, there are many valuable pieces in today's collection, which were transferred to the treasury as presents.

There is a throne at the foreground in every room of the treasury, which is composed of four adjacent rooms and among them, a balcony having an exquisite view. The throne in the first room was made in the 17th century belongs to Murat IV and it was made of ebony inlayed with ivory. Also, golden candlesticks and narghiles (water pipes), gold dinner sets, Indian music box having an elephant ornament, guns decorated with jewels, a walking stick decorated with valuable gems, which is the gift of German Emperor Wilhelm II, are in this sitting room.

The throne exhibited in the second room is a covered throne of the 17th century which belongs to the Sultan Ahmet I. Also, the famous Topkapı Dagger which was sent to the Persian Sultan Nadir by Ottoman Sultan Mahmud I is displayed in this room, since when the gift was on the way, they had got a news that the sultan was dead and it was returned to the palace.

Enjeweled ceremonial arrowcase (16th cent.)

The most interesting work of the third room is the Spoon Makers Diamond. This precious gem, whose name is believed to come from a spoon maker who found the diamond, is 86 carats and has 49 brilliants surrounding it. The gold candlesticks made for the tomb of Prophet. Muhammad and each of which were decorated with 6666 diamonds, are worth to be seen. The throne which Egypt governor Ibrahim Pasha sent to Murat III in the 16th century is exhibited in this room is gold-plated, made of walnut tree. In the fourth room, which is reached by passing through the balcony facing the Sea of Marmara, exhibits a gold-plated throne decorated with 25.000 pearls, which was sent to the Sultan Mahmud I by Nadir Shah. Bones of St. John the Baptist, prayer beads, jewelry decorated snuff-boxes, materials of writing, swords, works of ivory and tiled works are some of the most valuable works of this part. After the Imperial Treasury Department, we see the management units of the museum along the northern wall of the third courtyard, two narrow roads going down towards the fourth courtyard and two different exhibition rooms, which are not as large as the others. One of these is the COLLECTION OF CALLIGRAPHY AND PAINTING, where the hand-

Ceremonial Helmet (16th century)

58

written books, copies of renowned portraits of Ottoman Sultans, which are generally exhibited in the European museums, and Turkish-Islamic miniature paintings are displayed.

Following exhibition is the CLOCK COLLECTION of the palace. The most famous clock of the periods between 16th -20th century is the jeweled clock presented to Abdulmecit II by the Russian Czar Nikolas. Beside the clock collection is the exhibition of the HOLY RELICS which is one of the three biggest and valuable collections of the palace.

HOLY RELICS :

After Yavuz Sultan Selim conquered Egypt in 1517, he got the title 'caliph', which means the leader of all Islam world, and brought the holy relics which belong to Hz. Muhammad to Istanbul.

All the following Ottoman Sultans enthroned used this title. Sultan Murat III decided to display the holy remnants in the two adjacent rooms which were called Hasoda or Hırka-i Saadet Dairesi and used as a private room of the sultan until that time. In the first room, which attracts attention with blue Iznik tiles decorating the interior and exterior walls, there are drainpipes, locks and keys, and also swords of the four caliphs after Prophet. Muhammad. In a special display window in the second room, the jacket, the sword, the flag, the bow, the footprint, the tooth, the beard hair and a letter which all belong to the Prophet Muhammad are exhibited. The last work to be mentioned in the third courtyard is the LIBRARY OF THE

Throne of Shah Ismail,
Ceremonial throne,
Cradle of Princes'

Views from the holy relics' chamber.

PALACE located in the middle of the court-yard which was built during the reign of Ahmet III in 1719. Nearly 4.000 manuscripts of this library which was completely con-structed from marble are displayed in other collections today. Only colorful tiles can be seen in the building today.

There are two passages to the fourth courtyard which is the last courtyard of the palace. Going through the passages, we arrive in the TULIP GARDEN of the Sultans. Flowers of this garden are very pleasant especially in April and May. Sultans had the pleasure to watch the beauty of this garden

The Spoonmaker's (Kaşıkçı) diamond,
Topkapı dagger,
Ceremonial Canteen
Enjeweled glass pitcher.

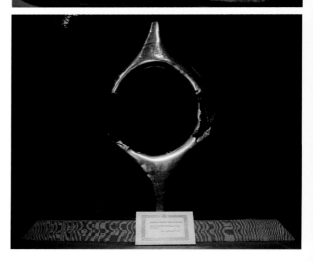

Baghdad Kiosk.   *Fountain of Sultan Ahmed III at the enterance the Topkapı Palace.*

from the balconies in the SOFA KIOSK to the corner of the garden.

When we go upstairs to the left of the garden, we reach the courtyard called Terrace of the Golden Horn. There is an exquisite panorama of the Golden Horn from this terrace. This is the best view of Eminönü and Galata districts and bridges of the Golden Horn.

On one side of the terrace is BAGHDAD KIOSK constructed during the reign of Murat IV in 1638, and on the other, is the SUNNET (circumcision) ROOM. Especially Baghdad Kiosk is one of the most elegant works of the 17th century Ottoman architecture with its blue tiles, gold plated dome, cupboard lids inlayed with ivory and tortoise shell.

End of the garden facing the Sea of Marmara there are HEKIMBAŞI ODASI and MECIDIYE KIOSK down the stairs. This building was the last constructed one before the palace was abandoned. It was constructed upon the order of Abdulmecit I by Sarkis Balyan in 1840. Preziori collection existed in the floral decorated building.

St. Irene Church.

St. Irene Church

S t. Irene Church for the first time was constructed over the remains of Afrodite Temple during the early 4th century AD. It took its last form after being restored by Justinian in 532. Before St. Sofia was constructed, the second Ecumenical Council was held here in 381.

It kept its importance as being the second largest church after the construction of St. Sofia.

St. Irene Church, with a cross plan, is the only Byzantine church in Istanbul whose atrium has survived. The mosaics of the church have the influence of Iconoclastic period (726-841). The building was used as an arsenal by Ottomans between the 15th - 18th centuries. From 1846 on it served as an Archaeological Museum. Today, St. Irene Church is used for classical music concerts due to its excellent acoustics. You can visit the church only by a permission.

Istanbul Archaeological Museum.

Istanbul Archaeological Museums

W alking down the street near the St. Irene Church, one reaches the main entrance door of the Istanbul Archaeological Museums, one of the five largest archaeological museums of the world. The Istanbul Archaeological Museums is composed of the Museum of the Ancient Orient, The Tile Museum (Çinili Kiosk), and the Archaeological Museum itself. The building of the Museum of the Ancient Orient was constructed by Academy of Fine Arts in 1883 and has the most distinguished examples of pre-Asian civilizations brought from Egypt, Anatolia and Mesopotamia. The most interesting work of this part is the lion sculptures from 14th century BC.

The Tile Museum was constructed upon the order of Mehmet II (the conqueror) in 1466 and it is one of the oldest buildings of Topkapı Palace. This building, which was used as an entertainment hall in the Ottoman times, has been used as a department where Turkish-Islamic tile and ceramic works are exhibited since 1967.

Archaeological works first gathered in the St. Irene Church began to be protected in the Cinili Kiosk from 1874 on. After the sites excavated in Sidon of Lebanon and in Konya, with Sidamara

tombs in 1887 were brought to Istanbul, a need for a new exhibition building arouse. Today's building was constructed by Alexandre Valaury in 1891 by the efforts of Osman Hamdi Bey, master of Turkish museology, and majority of the collections were transferred to this building. In 1991, the premises of the museum were put into service.

800.000 of 2.5 millions of works of art in all Turkish archaeological museums are in Istanbul Archaeology Museum. However, only one tenth of these works can be displayed. The works on display generally belong to Greek and Roman times. In addition to the tombs displayed inside and in the garden, there are many statues and other works of art in the museum. The cuneiform tablet collection having 80.000 pieces is the second largest collection after the British Museum. There are also nearly 500.000 coins from the Greek, Roman, Byzantine and Ottoman times. Besides, daily objects, oil lamps, busts, jewels, and many other archaeological works found in Anatolia and the countries which belonged to the Ottoman Empire taken to Istanbul are displayed chronologically and thematically in accordance with a modern museology approach.

A view from the Oriental Arts Museum.

Interior Views from Archeology. Lycia sarcophagus and Sidon sarcophogai.

Along the Sea Walls.

Along the Sea Walls

The old Istanbul is surrounded with walls built during the Byzantine period. These walls are called Sea walls along the Marmara shores, Land walls between Yedikule and the Golden Horn and Golden Horn walls along the Golden Horn. Total length of the land walls from Sarayburnu to Yedikule along the Marmara shore is 8,5 km. These walls were constructed upon the order of Constantine the Great in the 4th century and Theodosius II in the 5th century. The walls were frequently restored in the Byzantine period but ignored during the Ottoman period due to the impossibility of a danger from the sea. Only the walls, underneath the Topkapı Palace, were restored since they were used as walls of the first courtyard of the palace. There were important harbors and fishing villages along the walls. Many small and big doors were constructed on the walls in order to reach these harbors. There is no ruins in the region between Galata Bridge and Sarayburnu. SEPETCI KASRI in this region is in the borders of the Topkapı Palace. This building which is used as the Center of International Press is one of the three kiosks which are situated out of the palace and could have survived. It was constructed in the 17th century. The Bosphorus and the Golden Horn promenades of the sultan by boat began from this point. The building with minarets behind the Çatladıkapı District belong to SERGOOS and BAKHOS CHURCHES of Byzantine period, and known as SMALL HAGIA SOPHIA MOSQUE today.

A fisherman at Kumkapı and fishermen's taverns.

Kumkapı

Kumkapı, which is the first district on the coastline after passing Kadırga (galley) District which takes its name from the Kadırga Harbour where great galleys of the Ottoman fleet drew up alongside, attracts attention with its huge fresh fish market and fish restaurants. This district known as Kondoskali which means 'small quay' in the Byzantine period is one of the most vivid entertainment centers of Istanbul today. Visitors who want to have fresh fish and special sea food of Turkish cusine must spend an evening in this district. As in Kadırga, there are several churches in this district where Armenians were living during the Ottoman period. The first large cross-roads after Kumkapı is Yenikapı. Atatürk boulevard passing along the historical peninsula and reaching the Unkapanı Bridge above the Golden Horn joins with the coastline here.

This was the point where Lygos (Bayrampaşa) Lake was flowing into Marmara. Going further from Yenikapı towards the coastline, the first district we face is Samatya. There are many small and big churches like Ayios Theodoros Church, Sulu Monastery or Surp Kevork Church which was the old Armenian Patriarch, Ayios Menos Church and Hristos Analipsis Church.

The walls in the vicinity of Samatya sometimes go towards the left side of the coastline, seaside, and gives an idea about the natural coastline of ancient period. Narlıkapı, the last gate on the sea walls before the Yedikule Hisarı (castle) was the door used by those who came by sea to visit Studion Monastery right behind.

Yedikule Castle

*T*he splendid castle seen when we walk from the sea towards the land along the walls is the most magnificent part of the walls. It is said that Theodosius I constructed a VICTORY ARCH here before land walls were constructed. The arch which became a part of the walls when the actual land walls were being constructed between 413-429 became a place where important victory celebrations were made. This gate of 15 m. height, which was gold-plated, was called the Golden Gate. Commanders and the Emperor coming back from the victories in Europe and Balkans used to follow the road called Via Egnetia and pass through this gate called Porta Aurea with a magnificent ceremony, follow Messe Street and reach the Grand Empiral Palace with people welcoming them. In those period, there were golden and bronze statues on

Yedikule Castle.

The wall of Theodosius around Silivrikapı and a vegetable vendor.

the marble towers. This gate which was only used by the Emperor was laid with stones in order to facilitate defense in the regression period of Byzantines. There is another gate for people to go in and out of the city. Mehmet II (the conqueror), who ordered to be constructed three new towers in line with the others in 1457-58, evaluated this building as the next police station of the city, and used it for preserving the palace treasury. After the treasury was taken to the palace in the period of Murad III, it was used as a prison for statesmen and ambassadors. Lions of the palace were cared here for some time, then it became an arsenal, after being vacant for some time, it was restored in 1959 and became a museum.

Land Walls

*L*and walls of around 6 km. length were constructed under the supervision of Anthemios, governor of the city. The highest point of the walls strengthened by 96 towers were 76 m. above the sea level. There are 46 small and big gates along the land walls which provide connection with the city. There is a ditch of 20 m. in width and 10 m. in depth before the walls. Behind, there are two courses of walls the outer one of which is 7 m. and the inner 11 m. in height. There is a distance of 10 m. between these two rows of walls. Towers having 50 - 75 m. distance are 25 m. in height. After the Yedikule Castles come large gates like Belgrad Gate, Silivri Gate, Mevlevi Gate, Topkapı and Edirnekapı respectively.

The Region of Bazaars and Eminönü

T he region of bazaars is at the end of Çemberlitaş Square on Divan Road whose former name was Messe Street and which, begins from Sultanahmet Region, extends toward the land walls of the city. Daily life is dynamic here and there are several interesting buildings and works from the Roman, Byzantine and Ottoman periods. Now, let us pass from Çemberlitaş, through Kapalıçarşı and Sahaflar Bazaar and reach Bayezıt Square, visit Süleymaniye Mosque, and down from slope to Spice Market and take a closer look to the buildings we come across.

Çemberlitaş

N o traces of Forum of Constantine the Great, which was the nearest square to Hippodrome during Roman Empire, could be found. This square which, then, was surrounded with the senate and important official departments, today hosts buildings erected during the Ottoman and Republic period. The only work in the square remaining from that period is Çemberlitaş, known as the Burnt Column (Column of Constantine). On top of this column of 50 m. height, which was built in the 4th century with the instruction of Emperor Constantine the Great, was a bronze statue until 1105. The height of this porphyry column is 37 m. today because of the previous earthquakes and fires. The metal rings have been used to increase its resistance. Below its high pedestal, holy remnants which were brought to the city with the instruction of Constantine, like the pieces of the True Cross, the stone which Moses had broken with his stick and get water out of it are believed to exist. It faced an complete restoration in 1955.

Spice Market from the Minaret. New Mosque.
The column of Constantine the Great.

Nuruosmaniye Mosque.

Nuruosmaniye Mosque

I ts construction was started by Mahmud I, Ottoman Emperor, and after his death, completed by Osman III. It was constructed between 1748 and 1755. It is at the entrance of Kapalıçarşı. It is one of the most successful examples of European Baroque style applied in the Ottoman architecture. The mosque was constructed on one of the seven hills within the walls of former Constantinople. Its architect is estimated to be a Byzantine Greek, named Simeon. Some of the literature reports him to be Mustafa Agha. The most important differences of Nuruosmaniye Mosque from classical Ottoman mosques are the plentiful ornaments on the main walls, ornamented minaret caps and the niche overlapping the main nave. The semi-circle designed court-yard with 12 columns and 14 domes and without a fountain has architectural and ornamental baroque characteristics which the previously constructed mosques lack. The courtyard has three entrances and there are two rows of windows at the outer walls. The mosque has a single central dome and no column is present inside. The dome measures 25,75 m. height. The central nave has three big entrance doors. The central nave has many windows to provide a plentiful of light, as if referring to the name of the mosque. There are 5 rows of windows inside. The pulpit is made of green porphyry.

The Covered Bazaar
(Kapalı Çarşı)

Kapalıçarşı take the first place to visit in Istanbul for foreigners. Millions of different objects that are sold in thousands of shops seem charming for especially Western Visitors. Although it is far from its oriental appearance of nearly 100 years ago, it is still one of the most important places to be visited.

Kapalıçarşı has often been restored after big fires and earthquakes. Each time it has enlarged more and during the last century it took the appearance it has today.

Wievs from Covered Bazaar (Kapalı Çarşı).

Kapalıçarşı has faced 12 strong earthquakes and 9 big fires heretofore and the restorations after the earthquake in 1894 and the big fire in 1954 resulted in the most comprehensive works. Kapalıçarşı covers a total area of 30 ha.

There are approximately 3.500 shops and 15.000 tradesmen in 80 streets and roads inside it. Of the 18 gates of the Bazaar, the most important ones are Nuruosmaniye Gate which, on its pediment, has a rigging of weapon, book and flag and Bayezid Gate on which 'God loves tradesmen' writes and the imperial sign of Abdülhamid II is embroidered. Kapalıçarşı includes 7 fountains, one well, one mosque and twelve masjids (small mosques).

Covered Bazaar (Kapalı Çarşı).

The school and the bath were omitted during the restorations after the earthquake in 1894.

During the Ottomans, Kapalıçarşı had been not only a shopping and trade center, but also a place serving as exchangge offices and banks and where economy was organized. It was the vanguard of similar covered markets in Eastern countries.

At those period its streets would smelling spices, cloth or wood depending on the type of goods sold in the surrounding. Until mid 19th century, it had also served as a slave market. At the beginning of that century, people running away from the Russian revolution brought antiques with them and, as well as the valuable belongings of sultanate and dynasty, these had been sold in Kapalıçarşı. The first lace works, cloth and bed spreads imported from Europe were sold here at the same period.

Beyazıt Square.

Bayezid Mosque

*B*ayezıd Mosque represents an important transition since it is a combination of reverse T-plan of classical Bursa mosque and late Ottoman mosque architecture together. It was built by architect Yakup Shah or Hayrettin Pasha between 1501-1506, with the order of Bayezıd who reigned between 1481 - 1512. The main plan of the mosque resembles that of Hagia Sophia. This mosque is the first example Classical Ottoman architecture. Architect Sinan is said to have examined this building in details before he built his works in Istanbul.

There are three entrances at the front courtyard and three at the mosque building. There is an elegant 'sadirvan' (set of fountains especially for ablution) in the middle of the courtyard surrounded by 25 domes which are built on 20 ancient columns made of coloured porphyry and granite.

The harmony of red and white arches around the courtyard and the marble slabs coverings the ground are worth seeing. The beautiful main entrance door of front courtyard is opposite the niche and decorated with stalactite adornments with crown and epitaph.

Among all the market places established in Istanbul during the month of Ramadan, the one established in the courtyard of Beyazid Mosque was the richest and most showy.

There are two minarets with balconies at each end of the mosque, having 87 m. distance between each other. The one at the south has preserved its original form whereas the other at the north was reconstructed completely from its pedestal in the 19th century. The eight red braces on the minarets add to the beauty of the mosque.

The semi-domes at the east and west of the main dome are carried by 4-cornered main columns and 2 porphyry columns. The side isles are separated with columns and each is covered with four small domes. The adornments around the dome and semi-domes resemble cloth paint and remind the motifs of the tents of nomadic Turkoman tribes, ancestor of Ottomans. The tiles, engravings and old Ottoman writings inside the dome beautify the decoration of the mosque. The Sultan's Lodge made of marble is very elegant.

Behind the mosque there are three tombs. In the octagonal one made of coarse sandstone, Sultan Bayezıd; in the second his daughter, Selçuk Hatun; and in the third Büyük Reşid Pasha, the famous Grand Vizier of the Reformation period, who died in 1857, are buried. The charity establishment and primary school which belong to the mosque are today used as a library. The bath which was built out of old Byzantine construction materials, is kept closed.

Beyazıt Mosque.

Beyazıt Tower.

University of Istanbul and Bayezid Tower

T he building among the meadows behind the courtyard of Bayezıd Mosque and high walls is the Ministry of Military affairs constructed by the French architect, Auguste Bourgeios between 1866-1870. Before this date the Old Palace occupied this place. Old Palace was the place the Ottoman dynasty lived in. And before the Old Palace, there were basilicas built in 5th and 6th centuries at the same place. After the Ministries were moved to Ankara, this building was transferred to University of Istanbul.

The tall tower (85 m.) in front of the rectory building is Bayezıd Tower and was constructed in 1828 as a fire observation tower with the order of Sultan Mahmut II. The tower was constructed of white Marmara marble and its architect

Aksaray Square, Valide Mosque (Mosque of Queenmother).

was Senekerim Kahya of Balyans who constructed many palaces. It has 180 stairs and 4 floors. The names of these floors are 'turn, sign, basket and flag'. The neon lamps on top of the tower inform people about the weather and give meteorological information.

Laleli-Aksaray

D escending Ordu Street (former Messe street) Laleli Mosque of Laleli district can be visited. Opposite the street we see the Bodrum Mosque. It was constructed as the Myrelaion Church in the 10th century and converted into a mosque in the 15th century. The Valide Mosque in Aksaray Square is one of the most interesting works of 19th century Ottoman architecture.

Süleymaniye Mosque
Mosque of Süleyman the Magnificient

*I*t was constructed by Architect Sinan, the most famous architect of Ottoman history, between 1550 -1557. It was constructed with the order of Süleyman the Magnificent. During the reign of Süleyman the Magnificent, who has conquered Belgrad, Rhodes, Budin, Algeria, Temeşvar and Zigetvar, and who had conducted military expeditions to Germany, Hungary and Vienna. (1520-1566). The Ottoman Empire reached its largest borders. Süleyman The Magnificent had this mosque carrying his name constructed after 30 years of his enthronement. The reign of Süleyman marks the end of Ottoman Empire's advancement period. Süleyman reigned for 46 years and during these years the Ottomans developed a good deal in the fields of literature, science and art. Architect Sinan (1490-1588) is said to have worked using no plans. During his career, he had constructed nearly 400 hundred buildings. He was a son of a non-Muslim family from Kayseri. He was recruited and taken into the palace when 22. He worked as a janissary for 19 years and became an architect when his talent in architecture was discovered. He had similarities with Michelangelo, the Italian artist and also constructed many works outside the country, such as a madrasah in Mecca and a mosque in Budapest.

The construction of the mosque and complex was completed in 7 years. During the first 3 years, approximately 3.000 workers are said to have dug and paved a foundation to 6-7 m. depth. According to the construction reports of those days, 5.723 workers (of these 1.713 are Moslems, 3.523 Christians) completed the construction in 2.7 million working days. The cost of the mosque is $60 million today. The size and height of the dome Süleymaniye mosque is less than the Hagia Sophia's, but in terms of its general architectural elegance and size of the complex built in integrity with the mosque is much superior than all the buildings built before and after Süleymaniye. Usually non-Moslems were settled in this valuable region which is on the third of seven hills within the city walls. The mosque is at the slope of this

A look from Eminönü to Süleymaniye Mosque.

was planned to be deconstructed. The mosaics which were dedicated to Mary named as the 'happy mother of God' are the typical examples of the Byzantine renaissance, like those in St. Chora. When it was converted into a mosque the mosaics were covered under a white wash. And early in this century, they were cleaned and became visible again. There is a typical Byzantine dome over square plan of the church. The walls of the church were built of elegant stones and bricks.

The Kariye Museum or the Chora Museum

When it was first built in the 4th century it was given the name 'Chora' which means 'at the countryside'. After the expanding of the city walls, it was included within the borders of the historical city. But this did not change its name. It was built with the order of Maria Dukaina in the 11th century and restored and expanded by Isaak Komnenos. During 1316-1321 it got its last form by the addition of an exterior narthex and paracclesion (burial chamber). This last restoration was under the auspices of Theodor Metochites, a man of culture and art who spent his wealth for charity. In the early 16th century, in 1511, the building was transformed into a mosque with the order of Atik Ali Pasha by the addition of a minaret. Also, the mosaics and frescoes were covered under fine plaster in 1765. Kariye Museum is a masterpiece having the most splendid Byzantine mosaics. It is better to start visiting the museum from the nave which was the main worship hall. The colored marble on the ground and the marble slabs on walls create a nice atmosphere. Since, Ottoman period niche of the mosque

Chora Museum.
Mosaic from Chora Museum: Jesus Christ.

97

Chora Museum: Emperor Metochites is presenting the model of Chora Church to Jesus Christ.

had to point the south-east direction for the prayers of the Moslems, it is not at the center of the Byzantine apse. Right of the apse is the mosaic of child Jesus and Mary, and at the left one is Jesus Christ. These mosaics are partially damaged. But the 'koimesis' above the entrance door is well preserved. In this panel Mary lays in a bed and around her are Jesus, his apostles and angels. The most beautiful mosaics of the church are at the inner and outer narthexes. The diversity of subjects, richness of colors, the abundance of details in these panels are matchless among Byzantine churches. The stories depicted in the mosaics were taken from the Bible. But some of the subjects such as the birth and childhood of Mary were taken from Apocalyptic Bibles. The intention of these pictures was to teach the Bible, Jesus and his family to illiterate people. In most cases, the decorations of churches were drawn by the priests working in the church, but those in the Chora Church were the products of professional artists. These mosaics include vivid, realistic and dynamic scenes. Colored pebbles collected from the rivers of Istanbul and the coasts of Sea of Marmara were used to create these mosaics. The mosaics represent the revival of pictorial arts. In order to illustrate the third dimension in the pictures, the buildings on the background were drawn by covering cloth over these. The significant persons are illustrated from the front the others from the profile. The pictures in the mosaics follow a chronological order and the story begins at the left wall

98

with the annunciation of Mary's birth to her mother, Anna. Mary's birth, child-hood, presentation to the temple, marriage with Joseph can be seen in this sec-tion. At the each side of the door, which provides passage from the inner narthex to nave, there are the illustrations of St. Paul and St. Peter, and above the door is the illustrations of Jesus Christ sitting on the throne and Theodor Metochites. Depicted in the dome, to the right of the door, are the prophets and the saints from the Old Testament. Below this dome miracles of Jesus, such as healing the sick and raising the dead are depicted on the mosaic panels. In this section there is another picture covering all the wall. In this picture we may see the large scale mosaics of Jesus Christ, Mother Mary, Isaak Komnenos and nun Melanie.

The outer narthex includes a story which begins with the scene depicting the migration of Mary and Joseph to Bethelem. It goes on with the birth of Jesus. But later on the chronological order is undone. In the middle section the scene illustrates the temptation of Jesus by Satan. Just above the entrance you can see the miracles of Jesus Christ, the wedding in Cana and multipli-cation of bread. To the right side of the outer narthex entrance there are the part-ly damaged illustrations of Herod searching for baby Jesus and the miracles of Jesus. The section connected to the outer narthex with an L plan and separated with two columns is the paracclesion section and was constructed during 14th century under the auspices of Theodor Metochites. This corridor is 16 m. long

The Dormition of Virgin Mary.

and 5 m. wide. This section was constructed not to worship but to bury the dead. In this section are the tombs of Theodor Metochites, statesman Michael Tornikes and two unknown people, and there are frescoes instead of mosaics and theme of death is dominating the frescoes. At the end semi-dome of the apse of the paracclesion, you can see the anasthasis scene, which depicts Jesus Christ as he takes out Adam and Eve from the hell. On the arch in front of this is the illustration of the last judgment day and sinners being taken to hell. The central dome of the corridor was illustrated with Mary, Jesus and Saints frescoes.

The Tekfur Palace

T he gate near the mosque is known as 'Edirnekapı', as the travelers going to Edirne, during the Ottoman period, left from this gate. Going downhill at the interior of the city walls towards the Golden Horn, you would come across some Byzantine ruins.

First of the ruins is the TEKFUR PALACE, attracting attention with its different masonry. This palace is the only remaining section of the Blacherna Palace, which was built between 11th - 14th centuries. The building was used for tile manufacturing during the 18th century. Strolling through the ruins of palaces and dungeons, one gets to the Golden Horn.

Eyüp Sultan Mosque

*I*t was constructed in the memory of Halid Bin Zeyd, known as 'Eyüp El Ensari', who was martyred during the first siege of Constantinople by the Arabs between the years 674 to 678. Nothing has remained of the first mosque that Mehmet II had constructed. The mosque, visited today, was built by Selim III during 1798-1800 after the destruction of the former one during an earthquake in1766. The mosque has a square plan and a central dome. Around the dome there are 8 smaller domes. Its architecture is highly similar to the plan of the Sokollu Mosque built by Sinan in Azapkapı. It does not resemble much to the baroque mosques of the time. Interior of the mosque was decorated with calligraphic works and framed inscriptions given as a gift in different periods. The tile panels from the 16th century, dominated with shades of blue and green, attract most of the attention to the tomb of Eyüp Ensari. The building has an octagon shape and a dome. 'The Window of Life', which faces the courtyard of the mosque and has bronze carving, was build under auspices of Sultan Ahmet I. In the epitaph it is written that the Sultan Ahmet had also visited the tomb during the construction the minaret. At the outermost part of the courtyard and among the sublime plane trees there is an elegant fountain. In the three sides of the outer courtyard is a portico of thirteen domes on twelve columns. Of these domes, inner seven form the last congregation place of the mosque. There are small fountains called 'the Fountains of Fortune' at the four corners of the banisters surrounding the plane tree. Of the buildings in the complex of the Eyüp Mosque, such as madrasah, caravansary, hamam and soup-kitchens, only a part of the hamam and the tombs have survived. The boys to be circumcised, the hopeless patients in search for a remedy, the sport teams to play national games frequently visit the Eyüp Mosque and pray. In the Eyüp district, there are many tombs and complexes built for pious people who want to be buried in the vicinity of this saint. Moreover, it is very delightful to drink Turkish coffee by watching the Golden Horn from the Café above, the 'Pierre Loti' Café. The Cafe takes its name from the French author who wrote his works here in the 19th Century.

The Mosque of Eyüp Sultan.

Fener-Balat

*B*ack from Eyüp to the waters of the Golden Horn again, we can move towards to the city center. In the of Ayvansaray and Balat districts at the seashore, there are a lot of churches and synagogues. And the building by the coast is the Hospital of Balat which was built in 1958 by the contributions of the wealthy Jewish people for the treatment of the poor people. There are three significant historical buildings in the district of Fener. The first of these is the Rum Erkek Lisesi, which attracts attention due to its red walls and interesting architecture in the slopes of the Golden Horn. The history of the school can be traced back to the 15th century, and it has trained many high ranking people, and the building now in use was built in 1880. The second building at the sea cost is the Bulgarian Church. Its actual name is St. Stephan Church, and it was built in 1896. Finally, the Fener Greek Patriarchate, which is in the first street parallel to the sea cost, is one of the most significant buildings by the Golden Horn. The Fener Greek Patriarchy moved to the present building in 1602. Next to it is the Georgios Church, which was built in 1720. Some of the holy remnants of the Christians, the burials of the female saints, the throne of the Patriarchy and valuable icons are kept here. In the district of Cibali, which is the last district before the district of Unkapanı, is the Hagia Theodosia Church, which dates back to the 9th century and which was converted into a mosque in the 16th century and named as the Gül Mosque.

The Bulgarian Orthodox Church.

The Fener Greek Patriarchy.

The Pantokrator Monastery (Zeyrek Mosque).

The Pantokrator Monastery of the Zeyrek Mosque

The complex was built by the famous architect of the time, Nikephoros, under the auspices of Empire Johannes Komnenos II and his wife Irene in the first district of the 12th century. It comprises two adjacent churches, the burial chapel between them, the hospital, the old age asylums, the lunatic asylums and the dormitories for the priests around them. The churches were dedicated to Jesus Christ and Mary, and the chapel between them were dedicated to the archangel Michael. The Pantokrator Church is the second biggest church which has survived in Istanbul, following Hagia Sophia. It employed 700 personnel in its monastery. Gennadios, who was commissioned to be the Patriarch after the Ottomans conquered Istanbul, had been imprisoned here in the Byzantine era. After the conquest, the churches were transformed into mosques, and the monastery was transformed into madrasahs. In the following years, the buildings of the madrasah which was abandoned due to the loss of significance, and the church which was used as a mosque was neglected. The colorful mosaics on the upholstery and the colorful remnants of glass from the windows are the rare samples of the church's archaic magnificence which have survived.

The view of Galata from Eminönü.

Galata and Taksim

I n this chapter, we will try to identify the district of Galata, at the opposite side of the Galata Bridge, and the Taksim Square and its environs. This area which was under the domination of the Genoese and the Venetian in the Byzantine period, has revealed no remnants of these civilizations. The Galata Tower and the Arabian Mosque are most ancient buildings of this era. After the city had been conquered by the Ottomans, due to the principle of tolerance for the minorities, the region remained unchanged. Therefore, there are a lot of churches and synagogues in Galata, Beyoğlu and Taksim and their environs.

In the Ottoman era, especially since the 18th century and onwards, Galata and Beyoğlu and their environs had turned into an area where the European merchants and embassies were located.

The Tunnel

*T*o the opposite of theGalata Bridge, there is a short tunnel which connects the district of Galata with the district of Beyoğlu. This subway which was built between 1871-1976 by French engineer Eugene Henry Gavand, who after preparing its plan established a joint venture with the English businessmen. It is the third oldest and the shortest in length in the world. The subway, in which it is possible to travel 570 m. in 2 minutes, is now operated by the Municipality.

The Tower of Galata.

The Galata Tower

This tower at the slopes of Galata is visible everywhere in the city, and is 61 m. tall. The unique panorama of tower is one of the most important reasons why it attracts the visitors. The tower is at the hill which overlooks both to the Bosphorus and the Golden Horn and the Sea of Marmara. It is possible to ascend to the viewing terrace which is on the top floor of the tower, by 143 step stairs or by lift. It is known that there had been a tower in this region since the 5th century BC. But, the present tower was built between 1348-1349. The Genoese built this tower as part of the defense walls in the region which they conquered from the Byzantine, and named it as 'the Tower of Jesus'. The inner diameter of the tower, which has an altitude of hundred and forty meters, is nine meters. In the Ottoman era, the tower was used as a prison, warehouse, lighthouse and fire observing tower. It was restored between 1964-1967 and a new balcony was placed on it. The tower was the scene to one of the most astonishing events of the Ottoman period. An scientist named Hazerfen Ahmet Çelebi jumped down the tower and flew to the opposite side of the Bosphorus strait by using the wings which he had invented (17th century).

The Istiklal Street

*T*he street which connects the entrance of the tunnel at the upper end with the Taksim Square is called The Istiklal Street. In the late Ottoman era, this region was dedicated to the use of the Western countries for the construction of their embassy buildings. On this street there are cafes, shops and passages which had brought in the Western ways of trade into Istanbul at the turn of the century. There is a line for 'the nostalgic tram' operating between the Tunnel and Taksim, and no other kind of vehicles is allowed into this pedestrian street. The facade of the buildings on the street from the late 19th century and the early 20th century, attracts attention with the stone relief and human motifs.

Walking along the Istiklal Street from the Tunnel towards Taksim, it is possible to see, on the right, the consulate buildings of Sweden, Denmark, and Russia, the St. Maria Draperis Church, and the St. Antoine Italian Church. The St. Antoine Church was built between 1906-1912 by the architect Guilio Mogeri in the Neo-Gothic style, and it is the most important Catholic church of the city. In addition to these, there is Pera Palas Hotel, which is the oldest luxurious hotel in the city.

The Istiklal Street.

The Taksim Square.

The large space at the center of the Istiklal Street is the Galatasaray Square. The interesting sites of this square are, the Galatasaray Lisesi (high school), which is one of the oldest schools; the Post Office building dating back to 1875; the Çiçek Pasajı with several restaurants in; the Food Market, where every kind of food is sold; and the Galatasaray Hamamı, a typical historical Turkish bath. Departing from Galatasaray, on the left we came across to the Agha Mosque built in 1834 and the high stone building which has been used as French Embassy since 1920. Especially the cafes, pubs, and restaurants placed between Galatasaray and Taksim, are the most popular places for morning glory.

The Taksim Square

T he large square at the end of the Istiklal Street is the Taksim Square, which is one of the most active centers of Istanbul. This square which witness hundreds of people passing by everyday, is at the center of the commercial and shopping districts. The square derives its name from the building in which the water distribution for different districts of the city is administered, and which by the entrance of the Istiklal Street.

This building dates back to 1733. This square has witnessed many political meetings and demonstrations in the past. At the center of the Taksim Square there is the Republic Monument of 12 meters high, which was planned

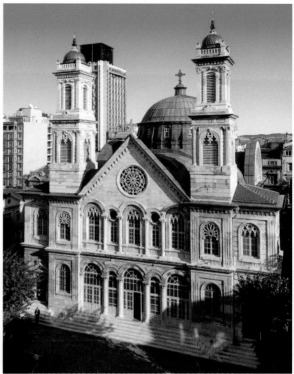

Taksim Square, St. Trias Church.

in 1928 by the Italian Architect Pietro Canonica. The ground around the bronze figures are decorated with green and red Italian marbles. The monument symbolizes the Independence War and the foundation of the Republic. The large building at the other end of the square, which was started to be built in 1950, and which entered into service in 1969, is the Atatürk Cultural Center. It was restored after the fire in 1970. There are concert and exhibition halls, and a cinema theater in it. On one side of the square is the five star The Marmara Hotel, and on the other side is a park area called 'Taksim Trip'. There were barracks in some part of the park. At the beginning of the Istiklal Street, on the left there is the St. Trias Church, built in 1880, which has a single dome and two bell towers.

The large street leading from Taksim to northwards, is the Cumhuriyet Street. On walking through this street toward the districts of Elmadağ and Harbiye; we come across Hilton, which is the first five star hotel in the city; the tall building used as officers' club, Harbiye Kışlası; and finally the Military Museum, which is one of the finest museums in Istanbul.

The museum, established in 1959, contains the weapons, helmet, uniforms, armors, and materials used by the Turkish army since 12th century till the Korean War. In addition to these, lots of paintings related to war, tents, flags, and pennants, medallions, the war spoils taken from the enemy armies are on exhibition (Mehter Musics are also performed by Mehter Orchestra in this Museum.

The Bosphorus.

The Bosphorus

The Bosphorus Strait, which separates Asia and Europe while connecting the Marmara Sea and the Black Sea, is 31,7 km long. The Asian cost of the Bosphorus is 35 km., and the European cost is 55 km. in length. The narrowest point of the Bosphorus, which has an average depth of 50-120 m., is at the point of Rumelihisarı and is 660 m., and its the widest section is at the point where it meets the Black Sea and is 3,4 km.

In the Bosphorus, there are strong currents on both directions with an average speed of 3-4 km/hr. The current flowing from the Black Sea to the Marmara Sea is at the surface, and the counter current is at 40 m. depth. The reason is the difference in salinity and elevation between the Black Sea and the Sea of Marmara. In bad weather conditions, the speed of the current can be to 8-9 km/hr.

The Bosphorus, which is vital for Romania, Bulgaria, Ukraine and Russia to reach the Mediterranean, and then the oceans, is an international waterline under control of Turkey, as mentioned in the Montraux Treaty (1936).

The coastline provides different opportunities to the citizens with several groves, tea gardens, cafes, bars, and restaurants, that are especially popular and crowded during the weekends and summer months.

The Bosphorus was formed due to the collapse of a fold line during 4th geological age, and took its present shape 7.500 years ago. Its name derived from mythology. Zeus, the god of the gods, transforms his lover Io into a cow in order to protect her from his wife's jealousy. But, Hera discovers the fact, and sends a fly to bother Io, and Io crosses this waterline in order to get away from this fly. Thus, this waterline is called 'the Cow (Bous) Gate (Phoros)'.

Throughout the history, the Bosphorus was an insurmountable barrier in front of the armies which wanted to cross over it from Asia to Europe or vice versa. The first bridge on it was built in the 4th century BC with order of Persian Emperor Darius, who was on a military expedition against the Scythians. The army of Darius of 700.000 soldiers, built a bridge by fastening the boats and raft with each other.

The Bosphorus, which contributed to the development of Istanbul as a trade center after the development of marine trade, was also evaluated highly in the Byzantine period and the first summer palaces were built at the cost line in this era. Some sections of the fortresses which were built in this period have survived to our date. The Ottomans had understood that it was necessary to control the Bosphorus in order to conquer the city, and therefore built Anadolu Fortress and Rumeli Fortress before the conquest. After the conquest, the Ottoman Emperors lived in those parts of the Bosphorus which were

View of Mansions by the Bosphorus Strait.

closer to the city center. With coming of steam ships to Istanbul, they began to live in the summer palaces, entertainment gardens and palaces which they ordered to be built at the distant shores.

Originally they were only fishing villages with no highway connections with each other, but timber villas and waterside residence chalets mushroomed since the sultans began to give lands as gifts to the high ranking officials to award or silence them. One of the turning points in the history of the Bosphorus is the year 1973. In 1973, first Bosphorus Bridge was opened, and Asia and Europe was connected to each other for the first time, the second connection was realized in 1988.

Annually about 50.000 cargo ships, super tankers, and big cruise ships travel through the Bosphorus, which is accepted as one of the most important, the busiest and the most dangerous waterlines in the world.

View of Mansions by the Bosphorus Strait.

Galata to Rumeli Feneri

When we start to tour in Galata, where the Golden Horn meets the Bosphorus, we can find out the natural and historical beauties on the European side. The Karaköy Pier, passengers harbor of the city, comes after the Maritime Lines management next to the Galata Bridge. The pier was built in 1894, and made it possible for Galata, which was the financial and trade center in the Ottoman period, to establish trade links with the world.

In the district of Tophane, the building left of the coastal highway, is the Cannonry, which was built with order of Kanuni over of the ruins of the buildings dating back to the Mehmet II's period. Similarly, the name of the district is derived from this early cannonry of the Ottomans. At the opposite of the Cannonry is the Kılıç Ali Pasha Mosque, which was built in 1580 by the Architect Sinan for Admiral Kılıç Ali Pasha. Next to the mosque is the Tophane Fountain, which built with the order of Sultan Mahmud I; this fountain was completely ruined as a result of a fire, and restored in 1957. It has a rich decoration.

Next to the green Tophane Summer Palace, which was built by English Architect James Smith in the 1850's, is the Nusretiye Mosque, which is one of the most beautiful baroque mosques in the city. The

The Bosphorus.

mosque has two thin minarets with two balconies, and a dome. It was built under the auspices of Mahmud II by architect Kirkor Balyan in the first half of the 19th century. After passing by Kabataş, which has grown into a center of marine transportation with the piers for ferries and sea-busses.

The Dolmabahçe Mosque

*I*t is the mosque which was built for Bezmialem Valide Sultan, the mother of Sultan Abdulmecit, by Nikoğos Balyan, the architect of the Dolmabahçe Palace and the son of the famous Armenian architect Karabet Balyan. Bezmialem Valide Sultan dedicated all of her wealth for the charities. The mosque, which was completed between 1852-1853, was built under the influence of Baroque and Renaissance movements. Its architecture is very different from the classical Ottoman mosques. Since it was designed as a part of the Dolmabahçe Palace, it resembles a highly decorated palace hall more than a holy place. It is so designed that it reveals its beauty more when it is watched from the sea side than when it is examined closely. The general plan of the Dolmabahçe Mosque consists of a single dome resting on

a square floor. The light from the large windows contributes to the beauty of the colorful marble decoration. The interior of the mosque is decorated with designs and embroidery, and the niche and the pulpit are decorated with European patterns.

The Dolmabahçe Clock Tower

*T*he clock tower, which was built in 1890 by architect Sarkis Balyan with the order of Sultan Abdülhamit, and which was placed in front of the gate, is 27 m. tall and has 4 floors. Its floor is marble, and the upper part is built by the stone blocks.. At its four sides, there are French Paul Garnier clocks and the royal emblems of the Ottoman Empire.

The Dolmabahçe Palace Museum

*T*his area was originally the bay where the navy anchored in the early periods when the Ottomans conquered Istanbul. Between 1611-1614, this bay had been filled in and a timber building with a large garden called 'the Beşiktaş Palace' had been built with the order of Sultan Ahmet I. The land of the Beşiktaş Palace, which had become completely useless due to a fire, was chosen as the site of the new palace by Sultan Abdülmecit I, since it was by the sea side and close to the city center.

Sultan Abdülmecit I, who was the 31st sultan of the Ottoman Empire and who ascent the throne in 1839, commissioned the Armenian architect Karabet Balyan by the construction of the palace.

The construction of the palace, which cost about 1 billion DM in today's figures, was started in 1843, and completed after 13 years in 1856. The Dolmabahçe Palace was an unnecessary expenditure for the Ottoman treasury, which had became totally empty because of the external debt. Since the collapse of the

The Clock Tower.

117

The Dolmabahçe Mosque.

Ottoman Empire, this palace had been empty intermittently for 32 years.

The last 6 sultans and Caliph Abdülmecit lived in this palace. After Abdülmecit, who lived in this palace for 15 years, most of the subsequent sultans preferred to live in the smaller palaces that they had built on their own along the Bosphorus.

With the declaration of the republic, this place was used by Atatürk. He used it as his residence when he visited Istanbul.

When Atatürk died in this place on 10 November 1938, after a long period of sickness, the palace was restored, its collections were rearranged and it was converted into a museum.

The palace, which was built as the imitation of the Louvre Palace in Paris and the Buckingham Palace in London in order to give a more European image to the foreign ambassadors and the high ranking European visitors, has a mixed architectural style called the Ottoman renaissance style. The marbles were brought from the Islands in the Sea of Marmara, the alabaster from Egypt, and the porphyry stones from ancient Pergamon city. The interior of the palace was decorated with the paintings, and ceiling illustrations were made by Italian and French artists. In addition to these, a lot of paintings by famous Russian painter Aiwazowsky enriched the interior decoration of

118

Dolmabahçe Palace.

the palace. It is said that 14 tons of gold and 40 tons of silver were used for the decoration of the palace. The furniture was brought from Paris, the vases from Sevr, the silk carpets from Hereke and Lyon, the crystal materials from Baccarat, and the candlesticks from England with special order. Almost all of 131 large and 99 small hand-made carpets are silk carpets, and they were woven in the royal workshops in Hereke.

The total area covered by the carpets is 4.500 square meters.

The palace consists mainly of three divisions: When evaluated from the sea side, Selamlık (Men's - administrative - Section) to the left, the Ceremonial or Grand Hall in the middle, and the Harem to the right. The functions of Selamlık can be compared to those of the second courtyard in the Topkapı Palace. It was forbidden for the state officials in Selamlık to enter into Harem where the members of the royal family lived. Similarly, the women and the children in Harem were not allowed to enter into Selamlık. The Grand Hall in the middle was open for both of the groups when great ceremonies, celebrations and admissions were held, but they had to sit in separate places.

The total area of the palace is 250.000 square meters, there is a 14.600 m^2 area on the same roof, and the total usable area is 64.000 m^2. There are 12 gates. The Treasury Portal, which is used today as the entrance of the museum, and the Sultanate Portal, which faces the main street behind the palace, reflect the whole splendor of the palace. There are 285 rooms, 43 halls, 6 balconies, 6 hamams and 1427 windows. In the interior decoration, 156 clocks, 280 vases and 58 candlesticks, most of which were placed symmetrically, were used.

The Selamlık tour starts from the Mabeyn-i Hümayun, passing by the Crystal Staircase, reaches first the Admission Hall, which is called the Red Room. The most interesting pieces in this hall on the second floor, are the ivory candlesticks, and the bear hides gifted by Czar Nikolaus II.

The silk carpet and curtains beautify the decorations. Next to this hall is Panorama Hall. It has a T-plan with a gilded ceiling, star-shaped interlocking parquets. One of the feature of this hall is that on one side has sea view and on the other forest view. The Music Hall, in which the musical instruments are on exhibition, and the Hünkar Hamami with its alabaster walls are the other interesting parts of the palace.

At the end of the tour is the Grand or the Ceremonial Hall with its 40 x 45 m. dimensions. The dome over the hall is 36 m. high, and in the middle of it a chandelier of 4,5 tons and 750 candles, which was presented by English Queen Victoria II hangs down. The hall is surrounded on three sides by balconies for the guests. There are 56 columns. The hall, which was used for ceremonies, feats and enthronement, was heated by a ground heating system for the first time. The carpet of 124 m^2 is the second largest hand-made Hereke carpet in Turkey.

Dolmabahçe Palace.

Beşiktaş

L eaving the Dolmabahçe Palace and walking along the shoreline we get to the Beşiktaş Square. This is one of the first settlements along the Bosphorus. There are a few historical places and two important museums to visit in this district. These historical places are the tomb of Admiral Hayrettin Pasha and the Sinan Pasha Mosque to the opposite. Both the mosque and the tomb were constructed by Architect Sinan. The mosque has a single minaret and 42 windows and was dedicated to Sinan Pasha, the admiral of Süleyman the Magnificent. Near the tomb is the Barbaros Monument made of marble and bronze in 1944. The height of this monument is 4.5 m. The first museum in Beşiktaş is the Fine Arts Museum inside the Dolmabahçe Palace and the other is the Maritime Museum. There was the Finance building on the site of the Maritime Museum until 1961. The museum includes objects, models, cannons, maps and uniforms belonging to the Ottoman Armada. Besides, there are three Orthodox and Armenian churches inside the Beşiktaş Bazaar. Moving along the shoreline, there is the Yıldız Park, a large wood. It was renowned with its laurel trees during Byzantine era. The Ottomans used this forest as an entertainment place and afterwards it was included within the Yıldız Park and villas were constructed with the order of Abdülhamid II.

Opposite to the park, there is an magnificent structure, Çırağan Palace, built in the 19th century and now is the Çırağan Palace Kempsinki Hotel.

Hunting Kiosk of Ihlamur.
Beşiktaş Ferry Pier.
The Palace of Çırağan.

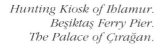

The Mosque of Ortaköy.

Ortaköy

O rtaköy is one of the most vivid districts of the Bosphorus and is an obvious indicator of the tolerance for other religions. Because a mosque, a synagogue and a Greek Orthodox church share the same district. The Byzantines used to call this area 'Arkheion'. The Turks began to settle in this area only after the 16th century. In the early 1990's the Ortaköy Square was reorganized and became a popular place especially for the younger people and students. The Ortaköy Mosque is along the coast. It was constructed by Nikoğos Balyan, between 1854 - 1855 with the order of Sultan Abdülmecid Khan. When the sultans were living in the Beylerbeyi Palace, they used to sail here with the sultanate caiques for prayer. In the streets at back of the mosque are the Ayios Fokas Church built in 1856 and the Etz Ahayim Synagogue. Near the mosque is the Esma Sultan Villa, built in 1875 with the order of Abdülaziz for his daughter.

The First Suspansion Bridge of Bosphorus Connecting Europe to Asia

Bosphorus Bridge or the
Atatürk Bridge

T he project preparations were started in 1950's and its foundation was laid on 20 February 1970. It was completed on 29 October 1973, the 50th anniversary of the establishment of the Turkish Republic. It was constructed by the German Hochtief and the English Cleveland Engineering companies. It looks like the Severn Bridge in England. Thirty five engineers and four hundred Turkish workers were employed during the construction. Its cost was $ 23 millions. Its length is 1560 m., width 33 m., the distance between the high carrying poles (165 m.) is 1075 m. The height of the bridge from the sea is 64 m.

There are 10.412 steel wires with a diameter of 0.5 cm. hang between the legs of the bridge. These wires suspend the bridge.

The Atatürk Bridge carries 200.000 vehicles and 600.000 people a day. It is the 4th of the longest suspension bridges in the Europe and 7th in the world.

Getting closer to the Bebek District is the Hidiv Palace, now the summer residence of the Egyptian Consulate.

The Fortress of Rumeli.

The Rumeli Fortress

D uring the conquest of Istanbul, Fatih Sultan Mehmet (the conqueror) intended to prevent the city get aid from the Danube and the Black Sea. So he decided that a second fortress should be constructed opposite to the Anadolu Hisarı (Anadolu Fortress). 1.000 craftsmen and 2.000 workers completed the fortress within an unbelievable time of 4 months in 1452. It includes 3 towers and walls among them. The name of the region was Hermayon and it belonged to a Greek monastery.

Near the seashore is the Halil Pasha Tower. It has 12 corners. Right of it is the Saruca Pasha Tower.

Its diameter is 24 m. and height 33 m. At the left is the Zaghanos Pasha Tower of 57 m. height from the sea. The width of the castle in north-south direction is 250 m. and of east-west is 130 m. In 1953, it was restored for the celebration of the 500th anniversary of the conquest. It has a cannon museum and an open air museum used for the concerts in summer period.

The Fatih Sultan Mehmed Bridge

T he Atatürk Bridge, built in 1973, was far from meeting the traffic requirements. Therefore, the Fatih Sultan Mehmed Bridge was constructed between 1985 and 1988. The opening date was at the same time the 535th anniversary of the Ottoman conquest of the city and the bridge is next to the Rumeli Hisarı. Therefore it was named after the conqueror. This bridge was especially planned to provide quick pass to the buses and trucks. Connected to the bridge is an highway of 216 km. length.

Emirgan-Sarıyer

M oving along the European side we reach the Emirgan District. There is the Emirgan Forest. During the Byzantine era this green area covered an area of 470.000 square meters. Its beauty increased with the construction of the Yellow, Pink and White Villas during the Ottoman period. It was opened to public in 1943. This forest includes more than 120 different kinds of plants. In the spring the Tulip Festival is held here.

The Fatih Sultan Mehmet Bridge.

Getting closer to the Tarabya Bay, there is the Huber Villa, which is used as the Presidential Palace (when the President is in Istanbul) today.

It was restored by architect d'Aranco. It has a grove of 64.000 square meters and previously belonged to Auguste Huber who had a significant role in the development of Turkish-German relations. Next to the Huber Villa is the summer time building of the German Consulate, the area of which was presented to Wilhelm II by Sultan Abdülhamid II. In the forest in back of the wooden villas is a German cemetery including 265 graves.

The Tarabya District is famous with its fish restaurants. Its name was Therapeia in the Byzantine period, the name was derived from the sick people coming here for its healing water resources and searching for cure, that was, a therapy for their illnesses in those period.

The private boat excursions on the Bosphorus end here and you may have fish for your lunch, then return

The Sarı Kiosk, Emirgan.
The Sadberk Hanım Museum, Sarıyer.

The Cove of İstinye.

to the city. When moving ahead, there is the Tarabya Hotel; the Italian, French, Russian and Spanish Consulates summer buildings, respectively till Büyükdere.

Between Büyükdere and Sarıyer is the Sadberk Hanım Museum. In this museum, the private collections of Koç Family are exhibited. The family is one of the most significant industrialists in Turkey.

Besides, the archeological remnants, there is an important ethnographic section reflecting the rich Anatolian culture.

The last station of the tours with the ferries of city lines is Sarıyer. Here there are beautiful fish restaurants inside the fish market. The remnants of old castle, temples and churches are in the Rumeli Kavağı, a small fishermen village, comes after Sarıyer. Here there is also a lighthouse.

This district is closed to ferry excursions because it is a military zone.

The Asian Side of the Bosphorus
Kadıköy

We may find here the remnants of the pre-historical settlements dating back to 4000 BC. We know that there had been a settlement here which dated back to 7000 BC before Byzas, the legendary founder of the city. The people coming from Megara had called the district which' s name then was Khalkedon as 'the country of the blind'. The current name has been derived from Khalkedon which means 'the country of copper'. The district was once the capital of Bithinya, a Roman State. One of the ecumenical councils was held here in 451. Kadıköy and its environs joined the Ottoman Empire a century before the conquest After the conquest this district was given to the administration of Hızır Bey who was a Kadı. Therefore the district got the name Kadıköy. As time passed, luxurious waterside residences and large summer palaces with gardens were constructed. Unfortunately, the number of these buildings have declined considerable due to the rapid urbanization.

There are no remnants of the past in this district. But Kadıköy and Bağdat Street should be visited to see that Istanbul has become a real European city. The Kadıköy Market has a dynamic business life through the day. There are many elegant shops and modern houses in Bağdat Street. Besides, the Armenian and Greek Churches that still continue their activi-

Kadikoy

Haydarpaşa, the Main Train Station of the Asian Side.

ties can be visited also. Opposite the Kadıköy harbor, there is the Haydarpaşa harbor, the largest import harbor of Turkey, and Haydarpaşa railway station, main station of Asian Istanbul. The harbor is insufficient to meet the intense city traffic. Therefore it is planned to be moved to outside the city. The 1100 m. breakwater in front of the harbor was built between 1954 and 1962.

The HAYDARPAŞA RAILWAY STATION was constructed by the Germans between 1906 - 1908 as an extension of Baghdad railway. The station including 7 rails and 4 platforms were constructed over the 1700 stakes installed in the sea. The architects were Otto Rittler and Helmuth Cuno. The pier in front of the station was constructed between 1915 and 1917 and is decorated with tiles. While moving ahead between Kadıköy and Üsküdar, there is the SELIMIYE BARRACKS. It is the largest military facility of the city. It has 4 towers at its 4 corners. It was constructed during the reign of Selim II. It was originally wood, therefore no traces of the barracks remained after it burned in a fire. It was restored with the order of Sultan Abdülmecid and its last form has been preserved till today.

The architect of the building is Kirkor of Balyan family. During the Crimean War, Florence Nightingale worked in this building which was then transformed into a military hospital. Near Selimiye, is the graveyard of the English soldiers who died in the above-mentioned war. The 'Karacaahmet Cemetery', located on a land between Kadiköy and Üsküdar, resembles an open air museum with all the grave stones from different ages. The cemetery was named after a Moslem saint. The cemeteries, on the Asian side of the city were preferred over those in the European section, as they were closer to the Holy city of Madina.

Üsküdar

Üsküdar is the historical residental area of the Asian city. In spite of all modern urbanization, the district still keeps its oriental character. The ancient name of the district was 'Chrysopolis', meaning the golden city. There are several stories about the name of the district. According to some of these stories, it was the golden color of the sea during the sunset; the gold coins paid as toll by the ships crossing the Bosphorus; or the gold that was forgotten here by the Persians after their Anatoilian expedition.

During the Roman and Byzantine eras, Üskudar was outside the city limits and developed as a military garrison. The district was named as the garrison in those years 'Scutari'. This is probably the origin of the current name. Üsküdar was embellished with different building complexes, financed and donated by the wives and the daughters of the sultans. The most important historical buildings are around the pier, however walking to the side streets one can still observe the social life of the past.

Üsküdar

The Mosque of Mihrimah Sultan, one of the two complexes that she had Sinan built, rises on a podium behind the pier. Mihrimah was the daughter of Hürrem and Süleyman, and wife of Rüstem Paşa. The mosque constructed in 1547 are among the earlier works of Sinan. The mosque has a dome that has sixteen windows and a baroque minaret.

The monumental fountain that Ahmet III had built in 1728 for her mother stands in front of the mosque. The fountain is a square with taps on the sides, and has the poems of famous poets written on. The second complex in the square is the Yeni Valide (queen mother) Mosque and its complex. It was constructed for Gülnuş Emetullah Hatun, wife of Mehmet IV and mother of Ahmet III in 1710. The mosque has a fabulous stone and marble workman ship, but very ordinary tile work. Among the complex buildings, there is a charity organization, a fountain, a school, and a market. Moving from the shore toward Üsküdar, we come across to a small but an elegant mosque. It is the Şemsi Pasha Mosque (Kuşkonmaz Mosque) built under the auspices of Avcıbaşı Şemsi Pasha, Vizier of Süleyman the Magnificent in 1580.

It has a single dome and minaret. There are two rotating columns by the niche. Architect Sinan constructed these columns in this way because the mosque was too close to the sea and these rotating columns served as warning indicators. The 12-room madrasah near the mosque is used as a library today.

Two Different Views of the Leandros Tower...

The Leandros Tower.

The Leandros Tower (Kız Kulesi)

The Leandros Tower covers an area of 1250 m² and was constructed 200 meters from the coast in the sea over some rocks in Salacak quarter of Üsküdar. The locals name it the 'Madiens Tower'. Both of these names depend on some myths. One of these tells that a Byzantine Emperor imprisoned his daughter in this tower. One day a witch got apples for the girl and gave her a poisonous apple, she died after eating it. That is why the tower is called the Madiens Tower (Kız Kulesi).

The name Leandros is merely an ascription. Because the relation between Hera, the Aphrodite' s nun, and her lover, Leandros, who swam here to visit her every night, is said to have occurred in the Dardanelles, not in the Bosphorus. But the same story is told for this tower also. According to the legend, one stormy night Leandros, swimming towards the light Hera kept for him, could not fight the waves and drowned. And his lover Hera committed suicide because of her sorrow.

The historical literature state that the war between Athens and Spartians took place here. Alkibades ordered a castle to be constructed here. And in the 12th century Byzantine Emperor Manuel Komnenos I ordered another defensive castle to be constructed. After the conquest, Mehmet II ordered another one and it was empowered with cannons. It was used as a lighthouse in 1600's. In the first half of the 19th century, during the Mahmud II period, it got its last form.

Time to time it was used as a prison and a quarantine hospital. It was restored between 1943 and 1945 and is now used as the Control Station. But plans are prepared to transform it into a café and restaurant.

The Summer Palace of Beylerbeyi.

The Beylerbeyi Palace

I t is known that Emperor Constantine had a series of entertainment places in this area Afterwards in the 16th century, during the reign of Murat III, European Commander in Chief, Mehmet Pasha, had a huge waterside residence, constructed here. The name of the palace comes from the title of Mehmet Pasha, the Beylerbeyi (commander in chief). After first wood palace burned in a fire, it was reconstructed with the order of Sultan Abdülaziz between 1861 - 1865. Its said that an orchestra was employed in order to harmonize the 5.000 workers. It was the second palace constructed on the Bosphorus and it was rather used to put foreign guests up.

Among its famous guests were King Edward VIII, Mrs. Simpson, Queen Eugenie (wife of Napoleon III) and the Iran Shah Nasreddin. Queen Eugenie is said to have liked the palace windows very much and wanted them to be copied in the construction of Tuileries Palace. The palace has three entrances and elegantly decorated. It has six big halls and twenty four rooms. The building is sixty five meters long and forty meters wide.

On the floors there are Egyptian matting and hanging from the ceilings Bohemian chandeliers. There are the most outstanding carpets on the floors which were brought from the weaving houses of Hereke.

In back of the palace there are magnolia gardens, a big pool and a few villas. Facing the sea it has a beautiful garden, a pool and two lovely villas. After being dethroned following the World War I, Abdülhamid II spent the rest of his life here. It is a museum today.

The Çamlıca Hill

Ç amlıca Hill is by the Beylerbeyi Palace and it is one of the highest point of the Bosphorus and Istanbul. It is 263 m. high from the sea level. It was used as a picnic area. During the reign of Murat IV, a hunting villa was constructed here.

The Çamlıca Hill has a wonderful panorama including the Sea of Marmara, the Bosphorus, the Historical Peninsula and the islands. In the early 1980's the Touring Automobile Association built a series of restaurants which include a Turkish cafe and a park. After the wedding ceremony newly wed couples come here to drink tea with their relatives.

The Küçüksu Summer Palace

I t was constructed by architect Niko-ğos Balyan for Sultan Abdülmecid between 1856 and 1857. It is near the Küçük Göksu River and has 2 floors. Atatürk also used it as a working office. It was restored between 1980 - 1983 and converted into a museum.

The area between the two branches of the Küçük Göksu River was a popular picnic place for the members of the palace and the people. The river, on which imperial caiques used to sail is far from its previous beauty due to pollution.

The Kiosk of Küçüksu.
The Bosphorus Shores (Kuleli).
The Mansion of Hidiv (Hidiv Kasrı).

Anadolu Hisarı (Fortress)

I t was constructed with the order of Yıldırım Bayezıd in 1393, during one of the sieges of Istanbul. It is opposite to the Rumeli Hisarı. In the previous period there was a Christian church at the same place. Its original name was Güzelce Hisar. It was very close to the shore when it was built, but this distance increased due to the construction activities which took place in the following years.

Around the castle, there are many villas constructed for the significant pashas and administrators of the Ottoman Empire in the 18th and 19th century.

Moving from the castle toward Beykoz, there are many interesting villas. These are: the Bahriyeli Sedat Bey Villa, the Zarif Mustafa Pasha Villa, constructed in the 18th century; the Amcazade Villa, constructed in the 17th century; the Hekimbaşı Salih Efendi Villa, the Ferruh Efendi Villa, constructed in the 19th century; the Yağcı Şefik Bey Villa, constructed in 1905 and the Hasan Pasha Villa, respectively. The last one is the oldest of these villas. This district is renowned with The Kanlıca yogurt which is sold in a cafe near the Kanlıca Pier. It is very delicious with powder sugar.

After this district of the Bosphorus, there are generally new settlement areas and at the end the fishermen villages in which fresh fish and sea products are sold.

The Stream of Göksu.
The Fortress of Anadolu
(Anadolu Hisarı).

Büyükada Island.

The Princes' Islands

The islands are in the Sea of Marmara. They, a few kilometers from the Bostancı shore in Asian side and twenty kilometers from the historic peninsula. We recommend the visitors, to visit these islands, especially in summer. These archipelagos are comprised of nine islands and two smaller rocky isles. They are called Adalar, but the foreigners call them the Crimson Islands or Princes Islands. In the ancient period they were called Demonesoi, that is, the Islands of the People. In the Byzantine period they were called the Papadanisia (the Islands of the Priests). In the Byzantine period the punished princes, nobles, priests and queens were exiled to these islands.

After the purchase of the ferries during the Ottoman period, the population of the islands increased rapidly. Generally Armenian and Greek minorities live here. The population was 1.200 in the 19th century, 12.000 in the 20th century, which rose to 20.000 today. This number reaches to 100.000 together with the daily visitors coming here in the summer season.

We may go to the islands with the ferries from the Sirkeci or Bostancı piers. Their names and surface areas are as follows respectively:

Kınalıada (Proti), 1.3 km²; Burgazada (Antigoni), 1.5 km²; Kaşık Island (Pida), 0.006 km²; Heybeliada (Chalki); 2.4 km²; Büyükada (Prinkipo), 5.36

Burgaz Island.

km²; Sedef Island (Antherovitos or Terebintos), 0.01 km²; Sivriada (Oksia), 0.05 km²; Yassıada (Plati) 0.05 km² and Tavşan Adası (Niadri or Niadros), 0.04 km². Of these, Sivriada and Tavşan Island are not inhabited. Kaşık Island is private property and Yassıada is used as a school. The others are open to settlement. The motorized vehicles are restricted apart from the municipality vehicles. The transportation is carried out with bicycles and phaetons only. Those who get bored of visiting historical places and want some fresh air and enjoy the sun and the sea may visit Heybeliada or Büyük Ada and have a phaeton ride, take a swim and have some fish.

There are the St. Yorgi Church in Büyükada, the Hristos Monastery in Kınalıada, the Priest School in Heybeliada, the Johannes Prodromos Church and the Sait Faik Museum in Burgazada are interesting places worth seeing.

Kınalı Island.

ISTANBUL

CONTENTS

Published and Distributed by

MERT Basım Yayıncılık Dağıtım ve Reklamcılık Tic. Ltd. Şti.

Cami Sok. No:42/B Osmaniye Bakırköy - İSTANBUL

www.mertbasim.com.tr / E-mail: info@mertbasim.com.tr

Photo : Güngör Özsoy, Erdal Yazıcı, Mert Basım Arşivi

Printed Turkey by : CEMTURAN OFSET Tel: (0.212) 567 04 79

© Copyright 2006 by Mert Basım Yayıncılık Dağıtım ve Reklamcılık Ltd. Şti.

All rights reserved.

ISBN 978-975-285-193-1